My
Road
Hockey
OBSESSION

My Road Hockey OBSESSION

CURT SOLOMON

MY ROAD HOCKEY OBSESSION

Copyright © 2014 Curt Solomon.

All rights reserved. No part of this book may be used or reproduced by any means, graphic, electronic, or mechanical, including photocopying, recording, taping or by any information storage retrieval system without the written permission of the publisher except in the case of brief quotations embodied in critical articles and reviews.

iUniverse books may be ordered through booksellers or by contacting:

iUniverse
1663 Liberty Drive
Bloomington, IN 47403
www.iuniverse.com
1-800-Authors (1-800-288-4677)

Because of the dynamic nature of the Internet, any web addresses or links contained in this book may have changed since publication and may no longer be valid. The views expressed in this work are solely those of the author and do not necessarily reflect the views of the publisher, and the publisher hereby disclaims any responsibility for them.

Any people depicted in stock imagery provided by Thinkstock are models, and such images are being used for illustrative purposes only.

Certain stock imagery © Thinkstock.

ISBN: 978-1-4917-5620-1 (sc)
ISBN: 978-1-4917-5619-5 (e)

Library of Congress Control Number: 2015900139

Printed in the United States of America.

iUniverse rev. date: 01/08/2015

Contents

Introduction

I'm just a dude that loves hockey, just like you. I've spent many nights watching it on TV, or in the rink, very much the same way you do. I enjoy watching highlights in the morning, reading boxscores, looking at standings, leaders, and schedules. I'm no different than you.

Perhaps what makes me unique is my *Road Hockey Obsession*. I know you played road hockey too. Our memories of road hockey are so palpable, aren't they? Picking up your stick with one hand, grabbing a ball with the other and resting it on top of the mesh of one of those light-weight road hockey nets, and then escorting the pieces down to the road. Where did you play? I put my net down on the street, right in front of my house. Once the net is in place, pop the ball off the top with your blade, and you're ready. There didn't have to be anyone else there yet. Take a step back and take your first shot. That first shot had to be effortless and natural. I think you and I probably both wanted to go top corner with our first shots. There's always been something about the top shelf that's endeared itself to anyone who's ever taken a crack at it, and it's not because the jam is there.

It always felt good to wire one upstairs and get the ball to bounce hard off the mesh and come right back to you. If not, the ball would sag into the onion bag and hit the hard road with a thud. When that happened, it was always fun to scoop the ball in the blade with just one hand on the stick and try to flip the ball upstairs from in close. This would happen a few times before once again stepping back to try another shot attempt. Did you go to the backhand? Harder to do, but so much more gratifying when you'd move to the backhand and sift the ball in under the bar. It made you want to try again, didn't it?

No differences so far. Maybe this is where I'll breakaway though. I did this almost every day of my life until I was nearly 20-years-old, and now I've chosen to write about it. Many hockey books have been written and published. Many I've read and owned. Seldom does someone write about road hockey though. Why doesn't it happen? I'm not sure. As we just established, you and I have played a lot of road hockey. It's something we have in common.

For me, road hockey was much, much, more than a pastime. It was the only pastime. When I started playing road hockey, I knew I had found the city of gold, and there was no use looking for or pursuing any other activity. How often did you play road hockey? I played six days a week, every week for ten months of the year, and for almost nine consecutive years. Add in a couple of games a week during the summer, and the extra hours spent playing on Saturdays, it's not inconceivable to suggest that I played close to one thousand hours of road hockey each year, or 11% of my calendar year. Now you see how obsessed I was, don't you?

I won't be offended if you're quoting Ace Ventura in your head. *"Obsess much?"*

Years of playing road hockey didn't offer me much in the way of hockey credentials. I'm not an Insider and I have no ties to the NHL or any player. However, I've spent so much time reading and watching hockey, and even working in the business as a reporter that I feel confident about my hockey knowledge. I've watched thousands of games, hundreds while in the stands. I've read millions of pages and have had long hours discussing hockey with like-minded individuals. You put me up against any one of those hockey pundits you see on TV, and I feel I could express just as much about the game as they do. I remember history very well and have a talent for putting names and identities to a place in time. I used to play a game where someone would read to me the name of a player who was traded for someone else, and I'd have to guess who it was. In other words, I'd get something like this, "This player was traded to Washington, from Anaheim in 1996 for Mike Torchia." It would sometimes take me awhile, and I wouldn't always get it, but I'd always take a good crack at it at least. (This was one of my favourite examples because I got it right. The answer is Todd Krygier.) I would just go through the rolodex of *Mighty Ducks* and *Capitals* in my mind from that season and pick a player I knew - or thought - had been traded around that time and try to recall if he ever suited up for the other team. It was pretty simple, but only if you'd read as many stories and boxscores as I did growing up in the '90s.

Although you may not have played as much road hockey as I did, or you stopped playing after you hit puberty, it doesn't matter because we still share those vivid memories of the game. Our sounds were the whip of the ball, the pounding of the road, the rough grind of leather on asphalt and the hollow sound of your wooden stick banging against the street. All of that, though long departed from our hands, still rings clearly in our minds. Road hockey didn't make us pro athletes, but it was impactful in our memories, just as those who were.

Preface

I've always enjoyed writing and so one day I decided to write about all the road hockey I had played. It was just a fun way to remember the guys. At no point was I contemplating this venture as a source of revenue or any part of a grand design. I just asked them to recall their favourite road hockey stories, and they emptied their memory banks. I owe the guys, first for playing so often and enjoying it so much with me, but also for hitting me with all the stories they loved the most.

I can't be grateful enough to my best friends who played so much road hockey with me. It really is a tremendous blessing and even a miracle that all of us, year after year, just played road hockey. We filed everything else behind our games. What an absolutely terrific bunch of guys for loving road hockey as much as I did and never making it feel strange to keep it going, well into our late teens.

While the guys were the biggest participants and proponents of my road hockey obsession, my family allowed it to happen too. I'm not sure if my parents just figured, "well, it could be worse" and let me have at it because all the road hockey was physically healthy, emotionally binding, and it kept me out of harm's way. I know, when I did things they disagreed with, they would straighten me out by suggesting I remedy the problem, or my road hockey would be suspended. That was enough to get me to adhere to their philosophies. They knew how much road hockey meant to me, and how much time I spent playing, and they were really good about letting me go and do.

CHAPTER 1
When Does the Game Start?

I can't believe there was a time in my life that I didn't care about hockey. It was a long time ago, but I can remember it. Before turning ten, my interests consisted of *He-Men, GI-Joe and Transformers.* I played a little soccer and Tee-Ball, but sports were not my thing. I am not sure why. My dad played a lot of sports - including hockey, as a young man - and he tells me I was invited to play hockey at an early age, but I turned him down... and for what? Megatron, Snake and/or Battle-Cat?! I'm not going to say it was a bad decision because I enjoyed playing with all those action figures, but let's say it was maybe, less effective.

Obsession is one step away from crazy, and I'm good with that. Do I have to admit it? OK. Yes, I'm obsessed with hockey. Recently, I got to hang out with an old friend whom I hadn't seen in years. I told him about this book, and he wasn't surprised. During our conversation, he received a call from his wife. He said, "Hey, guess what?

Curt is writing a book. What do you think it's about?" Without hearing her response, I listened to him say, "Yup, you're right." Even when it's been years between meetings, hockey is usually the first thing with which people connect me. I'm totally fine with that, pleased in fact. It's nice to be known for something.

Brantford, Ontario is known for hockey. A guy named Gretzky had something to do with that. Was it his influence in that city that brought my friends and I together to play hockey? Hard to say, because none of us were big fans of 99 growing up. Maybe it's just written somewhere in the city of Brantford's charter that all residents must love the game because Wayne put us on the map. I've visited Brantford's most famous, modest home and despite not being his biggest fan, there is something special about that house you can't deny. Gretzky's reputation is empowering, and his record book is motivating for anyone who plays the game in any of its fashions.

Hockey must have been in my destiny because it took a chance meeting between two fifth-graders to plant this obsession. Then in a span of less than a year, I converted from hockey know-nothing-at-all to hockey habitué. With little family influence, how rare was that? George Washington revealed the element for the Colonial victory in the American Revolutionary War was "Providential" care. I believe there was Providence in that fifth-grade encounter.

I had found my first great love and the honeymoon was on. I was like a machine and nothing else mattered. I just wanted more and more. (Boy, this really is sounding like a honeymoon now, isn't it?) I would watch and study games without guidance or aid. I learned how hockey worked from listening to play-by-play and colour announcers on TV. Another big help was my first NHL sticker book. This book had pictures of players, arenas, and at the back they even had stickers for referees performing hand signals for penalties. Even now, I remember studying those frames like someone would study history or geography to gain an understanding of their placement and meaning. That sticker book was a tremendous guide.

Studying was something I had to do anyways. Even in the summer, my parents wanted their kids to stay sharp, so we had to read every day and report to them what we read. While I enjoyed, *How to Eat Fried Worms*, I wanted to learn more about hockey. I didn't have any hockey books, so I went to the library. The first book I ever read about hockey was Grant Fuhr's, instructional goaltending textbook: *Fuhr on Goaltending*. Not sure why I picked that one, but it was helpful. I learned a lot more hockey jargon and strategy. However, I loved history, and I felt I needed to go well deeper than what Grant was telling me. I went to the source from which Google built its empire: the *Encyclopedia*. Although, maybe not as fast as Google, the Encyclopedia had it all. I simply found hockey among its vast volumes and pages and started to read. Each day, I learned new information about the origins of the game and its pioneers. I was enchanted by all of it.

Learning about hockey's past, made me develop a greater appreciation for those earlier rink rats. While my friends cheered for their contemporary heroes such as Ray Bourque, Cam Neely, Patrick Roy and Felix Potvin, I was teaching them the qualities of Newsy Lalonde, Eddie Shore, Clint Benedict and the greatest of them all, Bobby Orr. Bobby had retired from the NHL before I hit my first birthday, so I never saw him play. I learned about Orr from books, but also from *Don Cherry's Rock'em Sock'em Hockey*. Cherry had a little feature on Orr on most of those tapes, and I watched each show hundreds of times. Each Christmas I was given a new video and as soon as all the family had unwrapped their gifts; that VHS was rolling. Once I got into hockey, I received the newest *Rock'em Sock'em* each Christmas from my Grandpa Solly, who was a life-long *Maple Leaf*s fan. I always heard Gramps go on about how great Orr was, so I wanted to find out why. I read everything I could about the young *Hockey Hall of Famer*. The special Bobby Orr video that came out in 1994 was a wonderful tool as I got to see how Orr ran the game, scored unbelievable goals and took control of the games past, present, and future. I was awestruck. By the time, I was in high school, I had become the biggest Orr fan of my generation. Every player I grew up watching couldn't compare. One day when my kids ask me who the greatest hockey player was, I will tell them it was Robert Gordon Orr.

I would say most of us have fantastic memories of our childhood and adolescence. Those adolescent years were filled with new experiences that define much of our future characteristics. During those years when most other teens were talking about their crushes, listening to popular music, and creating memory-burning mistakes, I was pretty much missing out. It was true that hockey was on my mind 80% of the time. The other 20% was filled with family engagements, church responsibilities, my part-time job and school work. There was no time to go on dates because that was an evening without road hockey, and I couldn't do that! There was no time to listen to music because it would interrupt my reading of *Total Hockey*. I never attended a party because no one would be interested in playing road hockey. Some of the biggest movies of my generation never registered on my radar because no film could ever compete with road hockey. I never saw, *Schindler's List, Pulp Fiction, Titanic, Forrest Gump* or *Braveheart* in theaters (some of those I still haven't seen).

The amount of hockey history I got into had unintended consequences. Word got around high school that I was this hockey nut and that I was too obsessed. I figured, so what? Classmates of mine would ask me why I write names of hockey players on my binders instead of names of girls I liked. Some thought I was weird. Although I felt awkward answering their questions, I never felt like I was doing anything queer.

Let's be honest; I became very good at hockey history. A game developed around my hockey knowledge. It first started on the bus rides to and from school. Random people would ask me who won the Stanley Cup in a particular year. At first, I was apprehensive and kept to myself because I felt they were picking on me, but once I started answering, it became a game, and I was good at it. I could knock off just about any year proposed. The game evolved beyond the bus and into the hallways at school. Other students would say a year and presume I knew the question and I'd offer them an answer. Some would take coins from their pockets and read the dates off them just to see how many I could get right. I would be sitting there, in another conversation and someone would pass by and say, "1974" and I was expected to respond. (It was Philadelphia, by the way.) By my senior year, in 1997, I never missed an opportunity to educate a willing inquirer. The whole school was a quiz show, and I was the expert and the champ.

No question I enjoyed all the time I devoted to hockey and the attention it garnered me. Did I go too far? I don't want to say no because I loved it. If I was given the chance, I'd talk about hockey all day with anyone willing to participate or even just listen. I was fortunate that all my friends loved hockey too, but even they were a couple of degrees away from my obsession. However, I could have allowed more information to get through my hockey-filter. You see; hockey was so much a part of everything I thought about, read about, watched and discussed, that I missed some significant things. I cared little for actors, musicians, politicians and current events that could have really helped contextualize my life. For example, I remember sitting in front of my locker the day news broke about Kurt Cobain's death. Everyone was discussing it. Many were mourning. I had no clue who he was! It was April of 1994, and I was far more concerned about the NHL regular season ending. The Rangers were in first place and had a real good chance at winning the Cup for the first time in fifty-four years. Did Kurt Cobain play hockey? Nope. OK, moving on then. That was my thought process.

Another time this dude was wearing a *The Doors* T-shirt with a picture of Jim Morrison on it. He was talking about Morrison, and I asked him, "Did Jim go to school here?" This guy looked at me in stunned silence. Was I serious? Absolutely! When I received no response, I followed up by saying, "Did he go to North Park (another local high school)?" This guy picked his jaw up, waved his arms in disbelief and walked off. I didn't feel insulted; instead, I felt confused. Why would you bring up this Jim Morrison dude without telling me who he was?!

Millions of Canadians know what happened on October 23rd, 1993, because so many were doing the same thing. That was the day Joe Carter became legendary with his bottom of the ninth home run, sending the Toronto Blue Jays to their second straight World Series title. What was I doing? Not watching baseball that was for sure! I chose to watch hockey. I watched Toronto beat

Tampa Bay 2-0. It was the Leafs, tenth win in their first ten games of the season. That was significant because it set an NHL record (still is, although Buffalo tied it in 2006). I went to school the next day, and everyone was talking about Carter and the Jays. I was looking for someone who would talk Gilmour and the Leafs with me, but there were no participants. It was years before I even saw replays of Carter at-bat.

Maybe the worst demonstration of my hockey bubble was during the 1993, Canadian Federal Election. I knew nothing about parties, platforms or even those running. I was fifteen, and I had no idea who our Prime Minister was. The day after the election, our teachers were asking us what our opinions were regarding this historic election. I was thinking that I had no idea about what had made this election historic. Others began talking about seats, and I was totally lost. What do seats have to do with anything? As some poked fun at Kim Campbell's (now historic collapse), and laughed about it, I could do nothing but squeak out a couple of uncomfortable chuckles just to give the appearance I was following along. It was quite embarrassing to find out much later that Campbell and the Conservatives went from one hundred and fifty-six seats down to two in a day. That was a massive shift in Canadian politics! However, I was more focused on the huge topographical changes in the NHL landscape. Florida and Anaheim were brand new teams, while Minnesota had moved - of all places - to Texas!

Obviously, I was able to broaden my interests and began to follow more than just hockey. However, my hundreds of hockey books, which are currently caving in my bookshelves, may argue that.

CHAPTER 2
Let's Meet on the Street

It always started early Saturday mornings. I would wake up at 06:50, shower in eight minutes and pour a bowl of cereal in two minutes, just in time for *Sportsdesk*. I got into sports when I was ten and since then hockey quickly became my one and only. I'd sit in an easy chair about three-feet from the small twenty-one-inch TV we had in the entertainment centre along the wall. The early '90s graphics and computer technology hit the air with Michael Landsberg, Jim Van Horne or Teresa Hergert and officially opened the day with a greeting from the only, all-sports TV station in Canada. Fortunately, hockey always led, and that was good because baseball, football and basketball could only hold my attention if there was nothing else on. The hockey highlights would all be jammed packed into the beginning of a thirty-minute show. I credit all those shows for my terrific hockey memory today, because, on Saturday's, I would watch the loop more than once. I thought I had nothing better to do and no one else in my family was up anyways to challenge me for the tube. Besides, even if I had something else I should be doing, I'd probably still have chosen to watch hockey highlights again anyways.

I DIDN'T GROW much through elementary school or into my early teens. I was a small teenager, just barely five- and a half-feet-tall and a hundred and ten pounds, soaking wet holding a brick, when I entered high school in 1992. I grew up as a pretty active kid, but I was still one of the smaller guys my age. Size wasn't a reason I avoided more sports, but my size certainly did change my attitude regarding greater participation. Before hockey, my attitude wasn't about sports. I played but wasn't ever thrilled to be out there. I didn't drive the net in soccer, and I didn't look to hit dingers in baseball. When hockey sparked my sporting interest, I discovered drive, but even then, when I wasn't on the road with my friends, I felt outclassed, not just in size, but in skill too.

However, I wasn't blessed with some bound talent waiting to be released. When I finally picked up a hockey stick for the first time, in grade five, I played hard, and I never wanted to stop. I always heard professional athletes say the key to becoming a pro was hard work and a love of the game. I had both, but when you don't have any direction and you only play one year of organized ice hockey, suiting up for an NHL team will always be a dream, no matter how much you love to play. So, my game was road hockey. For nine years, starting when the silver ballet was first introduced to me, until the end of high school, all I did was play road hockey and plan to play more road hockey. Fortunately, the guys I hung out with were great guys, and all they wanted to do was play hockey too. We all loved road hockey. There was a core group of us, my five best friends and I. Luckily, we spent so much time playing road hockey that we never got into the bad stuff a lot of teens get into. Why would we want to do drugs or smoke? That would negatively affect our game, not to mention take precious minutes away from the black ice. School already took so much time away from our games; getting mixed up in troubles away from the asphalt was a distraction we never gave a second thought to. From grade five up until my high-school graduation, all I cared about was road hockey, and it was the best time of my life.

As much as it pains me to say it, I grew up a *Calgary Flames* fan. I blame timing. When I was introduced to hockey in grade five, the Flames were the best team in the world. I mean, they had Joe Nieuwendyk, Dougie Gilmour, Mike Vernon, Joe Mullen, Haaken Loob and my favourite player (then): Al MacInnis. A Presidents' Trophy season in Calgary made a young, unknowing person their prey. I latched onto the Flames and although letting this cat out of the bag sucks, who wouldn't cheer for a winner right off the bat? At least, I was still young enough not to get too sucked in. This is the kind of Flames fan I was; I didn't even watch them win the Stanley Cup that year! I didn't even find out until my friend Brandon told me at school the following morning! Despite my shortcomings to support the team at their most triumphant moment in team history, (and it's still that way all these years later) I remember being excited they won. I went home that evening and cut out the big colour photo of Lanny McDonald holding the Stanley Cup that was published in the Brantford paper and pasted it into my photo album. I also recall an article in *Sports Illustrated* that month titled: "Montreal Goes Up in Flames." IN YOUR FACE MONTREAL!

For close to ten years I was the lone Flames fan in Brantford. I wore their hats, shirts, coats and one very special gym bag. When I was twelve, I saved my money and bought a Calgary Flames' gym bag for twenty-five dollars. I used that bag for everything from grade six up until I graduated high school! I didn't care if I was their walking billboard, even when they frustrated the heck out of me. Calgary had this predictable pattern for years. A brilliant regular season followed by a do-nothing playoff. My friends' teams all had some level of success in the postseason, but aside from my first year following the sport, Calgary never treated me to anything more than regular season stats. Nevertheless, I was die hard. Back in the day, kids used to write letters to their favourite hockey players and I was no different. I wrote players from all over the league. Fortunately, many of them returned my letters with signed photos. The first player to write me back was Theo Fleury. Many years later, I bumped into Theo in his hometown of Russell, Manitoba and told him I wrote him as a kid. With anxiety, he said,

"Oh, man, I hope I wrote back." He was relieved when I told him he did. It's a special feeling for a kid to see their hockey hero's caring about them. I remember that emotion very strongly today.

AFTER WATCHING THE Sportsdesk loop a few times, the highlights on TV had gotten stale, and nothing else mattered. Once I had seen the hockey footage, the only thing I wanted to do was play hockey. However, most fifteen-year-olds weren't up at 08:30 on the first day of the weekend, so I had to wait, but for me, hockey never waited long. Even though I already knew the scores, I'd grab the paper and see if they had anything else to add to the hockey stories from the night before. Fortunately, Friday nights always meant a lot of NHL games, and there would certainly be a few stories and a pile of box scores to keep my attention for a half hour. I'd comb over the stats and keep archives. Now, to keep up with goals and assists is one thing, but I'd take it one obsessive step further. I'd track shots per period, special teams, penalty minutes and game attendance. I'd even compare the games with one another to see which goalie had the busiest night and which referee had the hardest time keeping the game on track. I'd write down the summaries from each game and file them into a binder. I did this for many years. Pretty much until the Internet became widespread, and I felt I didn't need to keep track myself anymore. The details meant enough to me that I still have some of those recordings today.

When I wasn't reading, watching or playing hockey, I still needed something to feed my hockey hunger. I would spend time covering every available spot in my room with hockey posters. I had so many! I even put up players I didn't really care for, but their posters were cheap, so I picked them up. Of course, I had my favourites, who in order were: Al MacInnis, Steve Yzerman, Pat LaFontaine, Alexander Mogilny and Roman Hamrlik. There were close to a dozen, large posters and a few dozen pictures I head torn out of hockey magazines. My brother, Neal and I, shared a room and he got in on the action too, helping to illuminate the walls with his favourites, such as: Mario the Magnificent, Kevin Stevens, Ronnie "Franchise" and Curtis "Cujo" Joseph. We would even cut and paste newspaper articles about our favourite players on the wall too. We must've had dozens up there explaining the qualities of either the *Flames*, *Pittsburgh Penguins* or *Team Canada*. Pretty much if it had hockey on it, we displayed it. We taped, glued, stapled, tacked and put hockey on every square foot of that room. The walls, both sides of the door, the closet, the headboards on our beds and the dresser were covered. Hockey was everywhere and it was just how I liked it!

Hanging and even re-organizing posters took up some time, but I'd spend more time categorizing and compartmentalizing hockey cards. If I could, I probably would have displayed them like my posters, but I had too much respect for them and understood their value, so I kept them concealed in their boxes most of the year. I remember when it was such a big deal to collect hockey cards, especially when *Upper Deck* started making them. Those cards were a few dollars a pack and hard to find. My friend Joel and I really got into the original Upper Deck series in 1990-1991 and had a friendly contest about who could get the set first. Fortunately for me, I had a secret weapon...my mom. Mom really liked going to garage sales. Every Friday she would look in the paper at the advertised garage sales and map out which ones she wanted to visit. I would often accompany her because I knew I could pick up some hockey cards along the way. Mom would help me by picking out places that were selling cards along with things she was interested in. She knew how important it was to be the first to arrive at a garage sale, so we'd get up at 06:30 on sunny Saturday mornings in July and August and hit the road. Shopping for hockey cards at a garage sale didn't compare to what you could get at card shows, but I picked up some good finds over the years. I once found a Felix Potvin rookie card, at a garage sale, and at the time, that was a big score. Another time, I picked up a Sergei Fedorov rookie card when I bought a whole case of mixed cards. Usually though, garage sales cards were an easy way to get commons to complete my set. For a long time, hockey cards would dominate my Christmas and birthday wish lists. One year my parents delivered this huge box to me for my birthday. I sat at the dinner table and opened it up. Inside was another wrapped box, then another and another. This went on four or five times until I discovered an Al MacInnis' rookie card at the bottom. I was over the moon at both the gift and the presentation.

Collecting sets became boring though. Everyone did that, and I wanted something more special. I remember the fun being sucked out of collecting sets when I found out everyone and their dog had the 1990 Pro Set. It drove the price down so much. You could now buy a full set for only ten dollars. Early in high school - probably grade ten -I stopped collecting sets and just started gathering cards of my favourite players. Now it was a real hunt to get what I wanted. There were always a couple sets a year by each producer, including special edition cards, all-star cards and trophy cards. This would mean I'd often need to find fifteen plus cards for each player, every year. It would drive me crazy to track down all these cards, but I also relished the chase. Many times I thought I had them all for the year, but then I'd discover more. Sometimes the card would be almost the exact same, but with one little thing changed, so I'd have to get it. *Parkhurst* made a set in the mid '90s called the *Emerald* set. All the cards in the *Emerald* set were the same as the previously released set except the *Parkhurst* logo on the bottom left of the card was a shiny, emerald green instead. It cost twice as much to acquire those special editions, and it was obviously a margin pig for the suppliers, but it hooked me in. I have hundreds of each of my favourite players and can say I own every single MacInnis, Yzerman, LaFontaine, and Mogilny hockey cards. Sorry Roman, I gave up collecting cards about six years before you retired.

I don't know how I had time for all this. My house was always busy. With three sisters and two brothers, things could get hectic, but it also meant a lot of hands to help work. I'd get assigned whatever the chore chart said. Mom's efforts to get everyone organized resulted in this large, coloured, flexible, bristle board schedule. You'd get one assignment a week. It might have meant dishes, and without a dishwasher, cleaning all the dishes from a family of eight wasn't the job you wanted. However, you could have gotten an easy one like vacuuming. The worst job was the bathroom. Females in the house automatically made it messy, and males in the house automatically made it filthy! On top of chores, homework, family meetings and even more family activities (like going to Hamilton to visit a seemingly endless line of relatives), I always had to keep my hockey time sacred. Visiting my relatives was the bane of my existence when I was younger. Only my cousin Sandy and my Grandpa Solly liked hockey, so what was I supposed to talk to everyone else about?! It would always be this grand occasion where every relative on my mom's side would get together (which would mean about twenty-five people in one house) or the same situation on my father's side, but with only twenty people, albeit in a smaller house usually. I'd think, 'Hockey would have definitely been a better way to spend my time!' Looking back, it's a very selfish thing for me to do, but that was how obsessed I was with hockey. It was all I ever wanted to do. To be clear, I do have many good memories of those family get-togethers and wish I paid more attention to them now that I'm older. I have my own family now, and I understand how valuable those family parties are.

CHAPTER 3
The Street Has a Name

It would be 09:00 by the time I finished watching the morning loop and reading the paper. Since I had been up so long, I figured all my friends must have been awake and chipper too. For a couple of guys, it was true. My oldest friend, Paul, lived six houses down the road from me on Dante Crescent. The day my family, moved in, Paul rode up on his sparkling, red BMX bike, and we've been buddies ever since. Paul and I were big fans of hockey early on, but even before that, we were big fans of the movie *Ghost Busters*, so I started calling him Venkman. He called me Spangler for a while, but it didn't stick. Thirty years later, I still call him Venkman. Initially, and all through elementary school we were a lot alike. We had similar physiques, interests, and skills; even our grades were equivalent (mostly B's with an occasional A and C). During grades seven and eight, we'd walk to and from school together. At lunch, I'd eat as fast as I could then hustle over to his house to play *Sega* for fifteen minutes before heading back to school. We'd usually play

California Games during those lunch hours (Go Thrasher). To this day, Venkman is still my oldest friend.

Venkman holds the longest friend title by just a few weeks. When third grade started, soon after we moved to Brantford, I sat behind Joel. Joel was also a hockey fan, but he was a superstar compared to me because he actually played ice hockey! He had already played goal for Tri-Church for a few years. Joel was a bright kid. He scored A's all the time in school. Also, he was athletic and nice. He was the perfect guy to sit behind as a kid. By the time I met Joel, he was already a staunch *Boston Bruins* fan. Even at a young age he would analyze wins and losses. His father obviously did a fine job bleeding the black and gold into his son. Joel's loyalty and devotion to the Bruins was already so deep, I thought it had to be hereditary; no one could learn to love a sports team this much by the third grade! Even today when I see kids, I don't think any eight-year-olds cheer for a team quite like the way Joel did for the Bruins back then. Joel was a big reason why I got into hockey because he was my first friend that had actually played the sport. Before I met Joel, I valued many things far more than hockey. Without question, reading *Garfield* and playing *Transformers* was much more important to me then. Fortunately for me, Joel was also a huge Transformers fan; in fact, we saw the original animated movie together back in 1986 (that was a heck of thing when Optimus died). His interest in hockey was a few years ahead of mine, so when we were together it was usually Transformers on the dance card. Although we didn't spend any time talking or playing hockey together back then, Joel's friendship was my first exposure to the game. Too bad that when we did start playing road hockey, Joel slept like a hibernating bear and would be in never-never land until late Saturday morning. How he slept so long is something I'll never understand. He knew I'd be calling him to play, yet he still wouldn't wake up any earlier.

Coons was the only other one of the guys who was always up early in the mornings too. Side note: I don't think I've ever called him by his first name; he's always been Coons. Coons moved to Brantford in grade eight, but we didn't become friends until high school when Joel brought him into the group. Coons was just like the rest of us; he loved hockey, but he also loved women. Without question, Coons' interests were a little more grown up than the rest of ours. While the other guys wanted to play road hockey - at least, I always wanted to play, and the other guys were the same most of the time, but they lacked the over-the-top obsession I possessed - Coons could easily be distracted by an attractive young woman. He was like a cartoon. If a good-looking girl came by, he would immediately become a rubbernecked dog. He would then go on to mention some brash, heralding remark about the girl's figure and how his contribution to it would bring joy to the world. Coons was never shy about what he thought, said or did, whether it was about hockey, school, girls and/or bodily functions. He delivered papers for the *Brantford Expositor* back then, but this is going back to the days when the paper was dropped off in the evening. He'd go out after school and deliver his hundred or so papers and then have to collect later that week. I don't know why Coons got up so early, probably to watch a little TV like me, but maybe it was because his step-father was a tool and insisted his fifteen-year-old stepson put two coatings of wax on his car by breakfast. Both Coons and Venkman were always up early and ready to go.

The itch to play road hockey was ripe. We had the whole day ahead of us, which meant we could play at least two games. Beside Coons and I, no one else had a part-time job in grade nine. I don't know how many ninth-graders have part-time jobs today. It's hard to say because fifteen-year-olds today look a lot older than fifteen-year-olds back in the early '90s. While Coons was literally up to his shoulders in ink, proving he worked hard, I was a "broiler-steamer boy" at *Burger King*. I'd place the frozen burger paddies and buns on a conveyor belt while the giant barbeque would cook the pieces until they dropped out the other side. I thought how it worked was cool, but I was so slow at it. The older teenagers that actually prepared the burgers for customers were much faster than me, and I could never keep up with them. That freaking steamer was always empty! Maybe it was because I was making an eye-popping $5.25 an hour. Rarely did I get off the broiler-steamer. I spent the first nine months of my working life there. However, this story does end happily ever after because it was the only time of my life that I spent working in a fast food restaurant. A couple years later, Venkman, Joel and a few other friends would spend much more time than I did wearing a grease covered apron and a funny hat. Suckers.

Since I was the only one who never stopped thinking about hockey for more than eight consecutive seconds, I was usually the one who initiated the games. It's invigorating to gather up your friends for a game. I found it very rewarding to formulate evening or weekend matches. I really enjoyed being the creator, but it never would've worked if, not for such willing and dependable friends. Venkman and Coons were always up early, so I'd make sure to call them first. I needed guaranteed players because I knew someone would inevitably ask, "How many guys you got?" These two knew I would call them first, so they wouldn't bother asking. I would for sure have three players, possibly four if I could convince my younger brother Neal to join in. Neal was four years younger than me, but he was a hockey fan too and so, sometimes I could persuade him to play. He was a lot smaller than us, so he really only ever wanted to play goal. When it was cold out, finding a 'tender could be tough. There were times, I, was forced to don the pads just to keep the game going. So, at least when Neal played we had one goalie, and to be honest, even though he was younger than us, Neal was pretty good. Even the rest of the guys noticed it. Neal could either stand on his head or be as sharp as a grape. He probably could have been a very reliable player if he had the desire to play more. Why didn't he? I'll never know. Then again, I've never understood why everyone on the planet doesn't possess the exact same high level of love for hockey that I do.

Although we were all close friends, we never talked on the phone. Calling friends just to chat wasn't something we did. Chatting on the phone only occurred during those rare cases when one of us actually had the guts to call a girl. When I'd call around to ask the guys to play, the conversation would be short, quick and to the point. For example:

"Yo, Venkman, it's Curt."

"What's up, buddy?"

"Nothing. Wanna play road hockey?"

"Yeah, what time?"

"Ten o'clock in front of my house."

"Kay."

"See yah then. Later."

"Yup, later."

After calling Venkman and Coons, the next guy I'd try would be Brandon. The Beezer was a lot different than John Vanbiesbrouck, with whom he shared the same nickname. Brandon was not a good goalie. What he was though, was another very reliable friend, although Brandon spent most of his time helping around his house. He was always cleaning, cooking, landscaping or doing homework. Incidentally, Beezer was probably the most well-rounded of the bunch. He was athletic, academic, clever, and had the most success with the ladies. Even though he was busy, Beezer would always make time to play with us. Hockey wasn't even his favourite sport (which I thought was a cardinal sin), regardless; he was still good at it. For years, Beezer was our scoring leader. Since we started road hockey seasons in 1990, Beezer led our many, yearly campaigns in scoring for four straight years. That dude was a point-producing, scoring machine! Beezer and I were stats junkies. The other guys occasionally cared about their points, but Beezer and I loved to monitor our progress. Counting and tracking goals and assists were vital to our road hockey games, seasons and years. We were both very methodical, organized people who valued structure. Maybe that was another reason why I was always the one who organized the games; I liked setting up events.

The only way you could stop the Beezer, is if he was in goal; then he was an easy target. His favourite 'tender was Tommy Soderstrom, a Swedish Sieve that enjoyed one good year in the NHL with the *Philadelphia Flyers* in 1992-1993. We loved making fun of those flash in the pans, never realizing just how difficult it would be to make the NHL, let alone from another country. We only looked at how good they were in comparison to Patrick Roy or Dominick Hasek. The same goes for Peter Sidorkowitz, Blaine Locker, and Jim Carrey, or at the time, Ronny Tugnut. Tugnut was our favourite to tease, basically just because we were immature, and he had a funny name. However, when we were kids, and Tugnut was playing for Quebec, he wasn't very good. Once he joined Ottawa in the late '90s, we were a little more grown up so the name wasn't quite as funny, and he wasn't nearly as bad as we remembered.

Well, Beezer may have liked hockey, but football was his game. He could play *TECMO Super Bowl* all day long. He could tell you what Barry Sanders' college and pro-rushing stats were for every year Sanders played. Despite that, if I called Beezer, he'd still play road hockey. Beezer was a leader and guys liked hanging out with him. If I got him, some of his neighbours on White Owl Crescent would join in. They were guys who weren't really our friends, but knew how to play, and when you're trying to get a game together, warm bodies matter. Aliens could have shown up, and if they knew how to play, we'd let 'em.

One of those neighbours; however, was a good friend of ours. Shawn: A.K.A Buff Dude, A.K.A His Royal Buffness, A.K.A Mega man. Venkman and I were thin. Beezer was short, but Buff Dude was both. The poor guy heard about this his whole life. He was a tetherball pole. If someone could get bigger by trying and wishing, Buff Dude would have been the biggest of us all! Unfortunately, bulking up with his genes, at this age was impossible. He was quick because of all the soccer he played, and he wasn't bad at road hockey either. He knew the game, but he couldn't finish. Buff Dude would get five breakaways a game and fail to score on all of them. Setting up Buff Dude was a gamble. You could feather one over to him, and he'd fan like a turbine. Beezer used to get so frustrated with this. He'd bang his stick on the road and scream, "SHAAAAAAWN!" or "UHRGAN!" Still, he was a big hockey fan that really had fun playing. Maybe it was his smaller stature, but he fought for the ball all the time. While I was reporting the play-by-play, Buff Dude was usually busy saying dumb things. We knew Buff Dude was trying to be funny, but like his breakaways, sometimes his comments left you hoping he'd get another chance to do it. It didn't matter what type of humour he attempted either. Coons had the perverted humour that made us blush because it was so off colour. Venkman had the goofy, childish humour. I was the accident-prone, victim of *Home Alone* kind of funny. Joel could produce one-liners from time to time that would make us laugh, but His Royal Buffness said things that made us laugh at him instead of with him.

Our talents were just as different as our personalities. There wasn't much communication that happened during a game, usually just fragments, curse words, sound effects and laughter. If anyone was going to be speaking, it was me, but it wasn't chit chat, and it wasn't water cooler stuff, it was the commentary. Like many Canadians, I grew up on *Hockey Night in Canada*. The whole CBC package was the best presentation of the NHL in the world. We all liked watching games and watching Don Cherry's videos, but everyone left the discussion about the game to the hallways, school buses and warm-ups. I couldn't though. I was so obsessed with it that just playing road hockey wasn't enough; I needed to be talking hockey all the time too. Naturally, I steered towards play-by-play. Everyone would be running around, going about the business of the game, at the speed of the game, but I would find the need to give my friends an earful of my radio voice while playing. For the most part, the guys allowed me to go about it. I'd go on for several minutes and was usually only stopped if something incredible happened (i.e. Venkman robbed me), if I couldn't speak for a moment (i.e. Coons knocked me on my behind) or if someone ordered me to pipe down.

Hockey play-by-play is the most challenging of any sport. It's so fast–paced, and there are so many actions, that it can be easy to get tongue-tied. Also, it can be difficult to remember names when you're calling a game. Although this wasn't a problem on the street, you could still get into the bad habit of excessive hockey clichés. All athletes use clichés. You can't watch an interview for more than one minute without hearing several of them. Some of the best players in hockey history can weave magic on the ice but can't come up with anything creative when they're asked to comment on it. The worst part of it is, we've all grow up watching these post-game interviews. Kids listen to their idols spewing out regurgitated, thoughtless lines, like a cliché vending-machine, and that's how they learn to talk about the game. Have you ever listened to young men talk about hockey? For the most part, they turn their brains off and churn out catch phrases. It's mostly because that's what they've been hearing pros do for years. It's a pretty relentless cycle, and I fell right into the cliché cave. I wrote for the high school paper, and looking back on those pieces now, I'm shocked by the amount of canned, useless conversations in there.

That was our core group, the six of us: Venkman, Coons, Joel, Beezer, Buff Dude and I. Obviously, there needed to be more. Like I said, we couldn't count on Neal all the time (lame). Getting eight guys was perfect because it meant three on three, plus a goalie. We'd try really hard to get Neal if we only had seven guys, but he wasn't interested enough if his presence didn't make or break our case. Most of the time, we played on Dante Crescent, where Venkman and I lived. We had some other hockey friends who also lived on our street that would play if we invited them. Across the street from us was a guy named Scott. He was a couple of years younger than us, but he had a good shot and was tenacious. Sometimes we found him annoying though, so we didn't really try to befriend him. We were just nice enough, so he'd play. We did end up calling his number most of the time, but it was always last minute. Since he lived so close, I'd just walk across the street and knock on his door as the goalies were putting their gear on.

Scott's best friend was this kid we called Curly. I knew Curly for years, and no one ever used his first name. He played baseball his whole life, and that was his game, but if we didn't have enough guys, and if no one was playing video games elsewhere, Curly would join in. Out of all the semi-regulars we had, Curly was usually the least interested, and not surprisingly, the least talented. It was embarrassing if Curly managed to get one by you.

On the occasion the miracle occurred, he'd whoop it up like it was a gold-medal game.

Then there was the man next door named Pierre. Pierre was a grown man, more than twice our age with a wife and twelve-year-old son. Since he had a family, job and other responsibilities, we couldn't really count on him, but because he was older and like a superstar to us, we'd always try to get him involved. Pierre randomly came to us one day while Venkman and I were taking shots (our term for practicing). He just burst onto the scene with his stick and started playing. Neither of us had met him up to this point, but he was the furthest thing from creepy, so we asked if he wanted to play with us when we had a real game. Pierre was good for a game or two a month.

For a few years, we had some fresh blood in the mix in the forms of Mike and Fumahiro. Mike's parents were brilliant enough to spell his name, "Mikle," which confused teachers at the start of every new school year. With a spelling like that, you'd always hear someone pronounce it how it looked, even though it seems pretty clear that the intention was Michael. Sadly, another case of bad spelling comes with everlasting effects. Mike grew up on baseball, but for a while we converted him to road hockey. He was our good friend for years, but after high school, he just kind of drifted away. Mike experienced a steady evolution to his nickname. Over the later stages of high school he was called: Mikle-Pickle, Drydick, Micky-D, MD, MD with the PHD, MD with the PHD in psychology, MD with the PHD in philosophy, geology, biology and so on. (Mike was the one who kept adding all those on by the way.) At last, after years of tinkering, we just called him: The Doctor. For the record, he was the best defenceman I ever played against. He blocked everything around him! He used a redwood stick, and he was pretty quick too. However, The Doctor had no shot, and I really mean no shot. Even when he'd tee it up, his shot was like a soft muffin floating through the cold air. If it had been just a bit slower, or just a bit colder, his shot may have just frozen right there on its way to the net. Nevertheless, he was still a guy you wanted on your team.

Fumahiro wasn't born in Canada. He came over from Japan when he was fourteen. Once again, it was Joel who befriended him, gave him a stick and voila we had a new friend and another hockey player. Obviously, Fumahiro wasn't going to be the name we called him for long. Unlike Mikle, it's a fine name, but we never called anyone by their first name. So, soon enough, Fumahiro was just Fumie. I don't know how, but Fumie was a huge fan of the *Chicago Bears*. He'd wear Bears' stuff all the time. I suppose he somehow watched Bears' games from Japan. His English was fine, and it improved the longer he hung out with us. He had never played hockey before he met us, but Fumie was a natural athlete. He was by far the fastest guy I'd ever met. He was like Usane Bolt to us. Even when he was jogging, he was faster than all of us. Beezer, Venkman and Coons were fast, but even they would be left in Fumie's dust during any one of the many foot races, which would occur during a game of road hockey. Once we watched Fumie catch up to Joel, who was riding a bike! How fast is that? We never taught Fumie how to play; we just put a stick in his hand and let him go. He picked it up just fine, and he was a great competitor. Although his stick handling took more time, he sure learned how to shoot quickly. When he would slap it, sparks would literally fly out like some kind of special effect. It must have been the force and angle at which he was hitting the pebbles on the street. Also, like The Doctor, he was an absolute rock on defence. You couldn't get around him because of his lateral speed and you couldn't dump it past him then beat him to the loose ball either because of his quickness. Fumie was terrific, but sadly, he moved to Connecticut in 1994, only a few years after he joined our group.

Those guys were my best options. The "A" team was: Venkman, Coons, Joel, Beezer, Buff Dude and I. The "B" team consisted of Scott, Curly, Pierre, The Doctor and Fumie. We even had a "C" team just for those desperate occasions when relatives were visiting, illnesses or alien abductions. The third-stringers honestly had some good talent. My brother would be considered part of that third layer because of his age and limited desire. Buff Dude's younger brother also fit in there, but for a different reason. Stephen was the smallest person I'd ever met. He was like sixty pounds when he was twelve! Keeping with tradition, Stephen also enjoyed a cheery alias. The evolution of his name was quite the merry road. It went from Stephen to Steve, to Beave, to Beaver, to at long last, The Beaver. Even though he was smaller and younger, The Beaver never backed down. I mean, you wouldn't feel much more than a mosquito bite when he'd hit you, but he knew how to battle. I loved having him on my team because he worked and unlike his older brother, The Beaver could finish. I don't know how he did it because his shot wasn't anything special, and he wasn't overly fast; he just knew how to put it where you couldn't get it. He was like a smaller Phil Esposito.

Another one was Kyle. Kyle was a loud, rambunctious kid with a temper. When Beezer brought him into the gang, in grade nine, I had no idea Kyle, and I used to be neighbours and friends ten years before our road hockey reunion. My mom found an old birthday picture of mine with Kyle in it. Mom had even written on the back of the picture, confirming it was Kyle. When I showed it to him, he was just as surprised as I was. It temporarily elevated our friendship, but Kyle was definitely the bad boy of the group. He ended up moving to Toronto in 1996, and no one kept in touch with him. Kyle's best trait for hockey was energy. He was short on skill and speed, but he never got tired. So, if everyone else had nothing left to give and Kyle was on your team, it was a good thing.

Two other guys named Randy and Jeff rounded out our entire roster. I don't even know their last names, probably never did; that was how little I knew about those two. The extent of our relationship was playing road hockey, and they'd only play if Beezer asked them to and if we were playing close to their homes on White Owl. Both were whiners, and Beezer seemed to be the only one who could tolerate them on a social basis. To the rest of us, they were players that kept the game going, and that was all that mattered.

That was quite a few resources for me when I was planning a game. Starting with Venkman and Coons, because, like me, it didn't matter what else was going on, they just wanted to get the game going. Beezer, Buff dude, and most of the others would get a call after those two. I'd have to call Joel last because he was always sleeping, which made it difficult to count him in. His sleeping-in seemed to represent his speed too. Joel was the slowest at everything. Dude was a good player, sometimes an incredible one, but his foot speed was often described by Coons as, "slower than death." Not only that, he needed like three hours to get ready. I can just imagine Joel lurching out of bed, taking a forty-five minute shower, eating a bowl of cereal like it was his last meal, and basically taking his sweet time at every mundane thing. Man, that would drive me crazy! I'd be forced to lie to Joel about the starting time just because we all knew he'd be late. If the game was set for eleven, I'd tell Joel to be there at ten. Even with this cover, Joel would consistently show up late, just as we planned. When I would call Joel, I knew he'd still be sleeping at nine, but I didn't care, I needed to play hockey and Joel's sleep was a minor inconvenience. God bless his parents for understanding because I'd call all the time to ask if Joel could play and if it was past nine, they'd always wake his sorry trash up for me. So, Joel would be half dead on the other line, and I'd be all excited trying to fire the zombie up for a game.

CHAPTER 4
Oh the Left!

It was 09:05, and all the core guys were confirmed for a 10:00 game. Things were getting exciting. In fall, playing road hockey was probably at its peak. It was early in the school year, so homework was minimal. There were still lingering effects of summer, so it was not freezing and we still had sunlight until late evening. We had six guys for sure, but we needed more. The Doctor was usually a good bet. Joel would call Fumie, and while he lived in Brantford, he was always in. Since it was a Saturday, I'd go and ask Scott and Curly to play before I asked Pierre (he was most likely working), but I'd check to see if his car was there when I passed his house.

Scott and Curly were like the Sedin twins if you got one; you got the other. The only thing that sucked about knocking on Scott's door was his father. His dad was a jerk who must have forgotten what it was like to be a kid, despite the fact that he had one. He always answered the door with a scowl on his face like he had just bitten into a mouldy, pickled onion. And although he wasn't a big man, he'd try to intimidate me by standing up real straight and sticking out his chest as if to say, "I'm the man, kid." It was really pathetic, but like I said, I was puny until the age of seventeen and so his mind games worked to a certain extent. I'd never talk to him; I just wanted his son to play because we needed him. On the other hand, Scott's mother was an angel. She was the tiniest woman, but also one of the nicest. She'd offer me milk and cookies and it wasn't like a "thank-you for playing with my son and including him into your plans" kind of thing, I think she was just genuinely nice and liked to make others feel good. Too bad Scott's dad answered the door most of the time.

Once we had all the guys we needed, finding a place to play wasn't hard. Dante Crescent was a long, "U-shaped" street, and my parents' house was right on one of the bends. We'd grab our gear and put one net right in front of my house and the other in front of Pierre's. This was a really small playing area! It was like forty-feet-long, just the width of the street and we were teens, not eight-year-olds!

Our road hockey equipment reflected our dedication to the game. Most of the time we used quality, second-hand ice hockey stuff. We also came up with our own actions during games that were unique to our group.

The foundation of road hockey was the net. Light-weight, plastic and small. It never occurred to us that we soon outgrew these frames. An ice hockey net wasn't an option, and we knew that, but we didn't ever look for anything else. As cheap as road hockey nets were, they did the job. We didn't go through too many over the years. The mesh however was another story. If there was one thing I hated about street hockey, it was the mesh in those street hockey nets. They were very difficult to put on, and I loathed the operation. The mesh would tear, creating big holes (usually in the bottom) even becoming completely detached from the net. A shot would go in, but then fly right through the net and carry on down the road. The celebration of the goal would be wiped out when that would happen because it meant a game of hide and seek between you and the ball. Many times -especially at night - we'd have to employ everyone playing to hunt, that spherical snot down and believe me, that ball would end up in the strangest, most unexpected places.

Then towards the end of the '90s, someone created a Velcro mesh. The user had to simply Velcro the whole thing around the posts. It turned an hour job into a two second job. Plus, the Velcro wrapping helped protect the mesh against the grind of the asphalt, earning greater longevity to the mesh.

Every now and then, we'd get real professional and use my sisters' sidewalk chalk to draw creases around the nets. They meant nothing except a point of reference for the goalies. However, we only did this when everyone was there, and the goalies were taking forever to put their gear on. It started with Venkman and me one day when we created our own pads from foam and cardboard. We designed them during a rainy day and made them look as professional as we could by drawing what real pads looked like on the outside. Once our creations were completed, we couldn't wait to use them and so, as soon as the rain stopped we geared up. Well, the cardboard lasted for about two minutes before melting on the wet road. Nonetheless, this sixth-grade project may have been the root to Venkman's attraction with playing net. I don't remember him being interested in playing goal before this, but I certainly knew he was after. Venkman quickly turned into a fabulous street hockey goalie. He certainly knew how to board up his net when I was shooting on him. We developed quite a rivalry.

It's hard to image that we used to play with a tennis ball. Those crazy things would lead to all kinds of missed scoring opportunities...kind of like today's composite sticks, only a tennis ball costs a dollar, not three-hundred dollars. We most often played on the road, not an outdoor tennis court or basketball court. The road had a bunch of tiny rocks, cracks and sometimes holes that caused that freakin' tennis ball to jump around like a Mexican wrestler. It made carrying the ball very difficult, and if someone got a piece of your shot, that ball was long gone and bouncing far, far, away. Beezer swore he did it on purpose, but sometimes he would fan on shot then recover in time to fire in a goal. I think it was pure luck when he did it (he even got me once). I was in goal, and Beezer is a left-handed shooter. He got a partial break, and we were using a tennis ball at the time. Beezer whiffed on it; I went down, and then a split-second later, he zipped it home, blocker-side. I can remember at that moment telling him how lucky that was, but he defended himself and probably still does. Come clean Beezer, it's been twenty years! The only reason we used a tennis ball was because it didn't hurt as much when you got hit with it. As we got older, and more serious about our games, we realized we had to convert. However, it wasn't until grade ten, in 1994, that we started using an orange hockey ball. Those things definitely hurt when you got hit with them, but they resulted in a lot less fanning and overall frustration.

Joel was one of the staunch opponents of the orange ball, and he had good reason to be. He was a goalie and knew that, that thing would kill if Coons or Venkman cracked one, and if he was unfortunate to get it in the bicep or thigh. Coons could really blast it. If he had better accuracy, he'd have been our Al MacInnis; instead, he was that Fulcrum kid from the Mighty Duck movies. I can remember standing at the side of the net one game with Coons on my team, knowing he was going to let one go, and I was just hoping for a rebound. Sure enough, Coons cranked it, but it sailed well wide of the net and beaned me in the head. Without a tip, how do you miss the net by that much?! My hat spun off my head while my life flashed before my eyes. This is why Joel would argue that there should be a no-slapshots' rule on the offensive side of centre. I bet Coons loved using the big shot because it gave him space and caused tremendous fear among his peers. The worst was when winter would roll around, and that orange ball would get harder than a frozen turkey. Then it would bounce, almost as much as a tennis ball and hurt twice as much when you'd get one. Years later, I learned to toughen up my shins using a glass bottle. I'd lightly tap my shins with the bottle and over time, they would harden up. I wish I would have known that trick in high school because blocking shots with cement-like shins could've saved a lot of anxiety.

In between the tennis ball and the orange ball were a few other experiments. During our early years of using the tennis ball, we noticed that the more it was played with meant the more fuzz that was shaved off, which resulted in even more bounces. Tennis balls would get worn down pretty quickly, and we'd have to retire them for new ones all the time. To reduce the bouncing, we would cut a small hole in the ball once it became too rambunctious. Then the ball wouldn't bounce at all. However, this only worked for a short time because the hole would grow and the ball would soon become a dead fish. You wouldn't be able to get any speed on your shot, and quickly the ball would split in two. For about two seconds, Venkman and I used a soft rubber puck. No question, it didn't hurt when it hit you, but carrying it on the road was impossible; it would often go on its side and roll away. The one day, we did try it, the puck rolled into the sewer, and Venkman and I spent hours trying to get the stupid thing out. We even created a device made from strings and tin foil to try to retrieve it; after that, we never used the puck again. When Joel and Venkman played in an in-line hockey league in grade twelve, we used a roller hockey puck for about as long as we used the soft rubber version. Pebbles and things on the road meant that the puck wouldn't roll very well, and it was hard enough to really sting when it hit you. Funny that Joel wanted to use the roller puck - which was very painful - when just a couple of years earlier, he didn't want to use the orange ball. Once we started regularly using the orange ball, we discovered we couldn't see it at night. When it was brand new and bright orange it wasn't a problem, but after a little while the ball would get scuffed and scarred and the colour would be diminished almost to, complete, blackness. So, we bought a bottle of glow-in-the-dark paint and painted the orange ball. It worked all right but not enough to make a difference, so we didn't do it again. Many years later, I saw a glow-in-the-dark road hockey ball on the shelf at *Canadian Tire*. We had the idea light-years before it was manufactured. We could've been millionaires!

Cheap pads and tennis balls were our elementary school playing options but that all changed in high school. By then, we had money, so we'd pool our funds from birthday gifts, Christmas presents, allowances and part-time jobs to buy new hockey stuff. We'd go to *Play it Again Sports* and buy some old ice hockey pads for eighty dollars and then use them until the stuffing was completely empty. We'd watch it roll down the street like dandelion spores. Duct tape quickly took over the leather look. Around the toes on the pads, it was several layers thick. That was easy to fix because we had all watched *Red Green* and knew how powerful the "Handy Man's

Secret Weapon" could be. However, replacing the straps on the back was impossible. After a year or two, many of the straps on the back were torn off, or at times only a couple remained. The goalies would have to criss-cross the straps to make up for the lost real estate on their legs. It worked pretty well, but it was inevitable that one of those pads would spin around on their leg and going down could have meant an unwanted meeting between patella and pavement. Sometimes we would use the duct tape to tape the entire pad on a leg so this could be avoided. This meant that we would have to cut off the pad after each game. It was really annoying, especially if one guy started in goal, but didn't fare well and wanted out quickly. We sure worked those pads hard.

Between cardboard and ice hockey pads, we had these hard, plastic *Cooper* pads. They were made to be durable, and they certainly accomplished that. We could walk around the block on our knees in these things, and they wouldn't show even the slightest tear. They were awesome for about a day...and then we actually used them. They were soft enough so that you could bend your knees, but you couldn't move laterally very well. They were bulky and awkward which made getting up and doing down in them quite difficult. But, the worst feature about these was the rebounds. Anything that hit these plastic walls bounced back like a proton in a particle accelerator. Some of us learned to really boot shots away if we could and keep those rebounds away from the front of the net. Other times, though, in close, you couldn't do that and depositing rebounds was like picking cherries.

I don't remember who did it or when, but whoever discovered using hockey pants for playing goal in road hockey was a genius! I don't know how we ever played goal without hockey pants, yet we did it for so long. Pants gave us courage in net by protecting our thighs from shots and our butts from the grind against the asphalt. For some bizarre reason, we only started wearing cups, after we started wearing pants. What was that about? I know that by the time we were seventeen and eighteen years old, we clued in, and started taking the very best care of our junk, but I don't know why we didn't at fifteen. Maybe it was because we hadn't figured out that boxers were better than briefs yet either.

Sadly for Venkman, protecting his jewels was a constant test. Venkman was a good goalie, probably, the best one among us. So, maybe it was the amount of time he spent in net that made him a constant sack causality. Probably ten times a month, Venkman would get bagged and topple over faster than a row of dominoes. It wasn't just getting squared for Venkman, it was either some terrible (yet, extremely hilarious) fate or some awful (yet again, hilarious) luck, but Venkman was always getting these shots in the same spot. He coined the phrase, "OH THE LEFT!" because these repeated attacks savagely targeted his left nut. I feel bad for him now because it happened...all the time! For years, none of us wore cups, and we all played enough to get squared once in a while, but poor Venkman suffered a lot more than all of us combined. During all those years of ball hockey bag barrage, it was always so funny to stop and watch as Venkman hit the dirt. We'd all rolled around in uncontrollable teenage laughter. I know it's not funny when you get hit, but man it's a riot when you see someone else get it! You'd think we'd be more sympathetic, but we weren't. Remember Homer laughing hysterically at Hans Moleman in "Man Getting Hit by Football"? That was us every time Venkman caught a third ball.

Of course, when you were playing any game, the possibility of getting squared was real. Six to ten guys running around with sticks, shooting a ball at one another, it was only a matter of time. Like I said, Venkman got it the worst, or at least the most, which you could argue was the worst. With him and Joel in net most of the time, those two had the highest risk, but they also enjoyed the most protection. I know sometimes when Venkman did get bagged; he was wearing a jock, but would still make the contact known ("Oh the left!) and drop down. For the rest of us (not wearing cups), taking a shot in the junk was always an awful time. Occasionally, we would play on the parking lot of our old elementary school. It was a ten-minute walk, but it wasn't easy having to carry the nets, sticks and equipment on our shoulders. The "tarvia" – as the teachers called it when we were kids - had cracks in it that had been filled with a kind of black gum as a repairing agent. On a hot day, that stuff was pliable and a little sticky. One time, I was unfortunate enough to experience the bad luck of getting stuck in it. I was running with my stick facing downwards, and the tip of my blade got jammed into the black filler stopping my progression instantly. My body's momentum kept me going, and the butt end of my stick drove right into my package at full force. I thought I was going to puke and die! I did my best to hide the pain, but it was impossible. I almost blacked out from the agony. I was laying on my side, holding my boys and rocking back and forth in a way to sooth the thing that could not be. My nuts were driven up so far into my gut that I had to wait until I farted to feel semi-normal again. Why is it when you get hit in the balls you fart after?

The best junk shot had to have been Coons' though. When he first started playing with us in 1992, Coons was always a goalie and a good one at that. Nevertheless, he stopped playing net after just one year and rarely attended goal again. He said he "just didn't care to do it anymore." One time though – a few years after his decision to hang up the pads - he decided to strap 'em on as we were warming up to play Beal's team.

It was pretty lame that all of us would play this guy and his friends. Beal and his buddies were all at least five years younger than us, but somehow or another, Joel hooked us up and we played these kids a few times. Obviously, we were so desperate to play road hockey that we'd play anyone.

So, we were warming Coons up (he was not wearing the hockey pants), and as we all soon found out, he wasn't wearing a jock either. Venkman could really shoot it and although he wasn't trying to hurt Coons, he fired one from about seven-feet out and for some reason, Coons stretched out, fully exposing his jewels as he attempted to stop the shot. I was standing on Coons' right and watched - like it was in slow motion – the ball slam right into him. The holler Coons let out, still resides in my memory today. I saw every muscle on his face contort as he fell backwards. Right away, Venkman doubled over laughing. Coons was face down on the street, and if he hadn't just been sacked, I'm pretty sure he would've killed Venkman that day. Whenever Coons got upset, he would swear a lot. He already had the worst language of anyone I knew, but his curse words went to another level when he was mad, and it was intimidating. Despite all this, I was on the verge of cracking up myself. While undoing his gear, I was struggling to hold my bubbling laughter in, but I knew if I didn't, I'd regret it. It's just so freaking funny to see someone get bagged then struggle to do anything for the next few minutes.

Along with hockey pants, our goalies also began to wear shoulder pads for chest protection. We never had professional goaltender pads that covered the goalie's entire torso and arms; we used old player shoulder pads, the kind of pads skaters used in the '50s. Before this, our poor goalies would just layer up on sweaters, hoodies and coats to soften the pain of body shots. In the winter, this wasn't the worst plan, but in the summer when the rest of us would be running around in shorts, the goalies would still be piling on the layers like an Eskimo on the frozen tundra. Although it wasn't full protection, it was nice to know our goalies were a little more relaxed about taking those high shots without growing their contusion collection.

Hand protection was pretty simple. Goalie trappers were expensive, and although they captured our imaginations, we usually only had one and it would get torn up pretty badly. Duct tape worked best on straight lines, but trappers had so many curves, and so the tape didn't work very well with them. However, finding a replacement was easy because everyone had a baseball glove. In all those years of road hockey, I think we owned two real trappers, the rest of the time we used ball gloves.

The Doctor was always more of a baseball player than a road hockey player. I can remember during the summer between grades eight and nine, The Doctor sparked a tradition that lasted for a few years. We'd give up road hockey for July and August and play baseball at the brand-new diamonds on Dunsdon Road. These fields had a well-maintained infield, a large outfield and best of all, a fence! None of us could ever hit a homer during a real game, but Joel hit the top of the fence once, and that was impressive. Even though The Doctor convinced us to give up road hockey for two months, we converted him to road hockey for the other ten months. He played with us all the time during the last three years of high school. He actually became quite a reliable player. He could always make us laugh (either by what he said or how he moved). He had this very awkward way of stick handling and carrying the ball. The Doctor was definitely the stay-at-home defenceman of the group. He and Fumie could stop a rush, but they couldn't start one. Every now and then – just for fun – The Doctor would strap 'em on and tend goal. Although he always insisted on using a ball glove instead of a trapper, a ski glove instead of a blocker and a regular stick instead of a goalie stick. Picture this for a second. The Doctor. A tall, thin dude playing net with an old ball glove, a beat up ski mitt and a regular hockey stick. No wonder he wasn't very good in goal, he was like a cheap furnace filter offering so little protection. He used to joke about needing a fourteen goal warm up. Maybe he already stunk, and it wouldn't matter if he dressed up like Garth Snow because he wasn't stopping much. At least the ball glove probably made him feel like he could still practice baseball while in the off season.

Blockers were cheap and tough so getting a couple of those was easy. However, like the pads and trappers, the straps would be one of the first things to break and so we'd either have to duct tape around the hand or use the old ski glove instead. Also, the palm in the blocker would always disintegrate and so the goalie would be forced to wear a ski glove just to keep the blocker on his hand. When we didn't have a blocker, it was just a ski glove. Although it didn't cover the net like a blocker, it saved your hand. You could stop shots and cover the ball up in a scramble with the glove without getting hurt.

Goalie sticks were expensive, and because we could just use a regular stick, it wasn't something we all felt we needed. Joel and Venkman were our usual goalies and thus the two who argued they needed a big stick to command the net. Due to their higher price tag, whenever a goalie stick would break, we'd use any means necessary to keep it going. We would tape the shattered piece back on, glue in those plastic blades or as a preventative measure, we'd cover the whole thing up in layers of duct tape. The stick was almost impossible to manoeuvre because the tape prevented your hand from sliding up and down the shaft, but we'd get an extra six months out of it.

On top of it, all was the mask. Although his time in goal was brief, Coons left his mark on the position. He was the Jacque Plante among us, being the first to wear a goalie mask. (Yes, I know Clint Benedict wore a mask before Plante, but Plante gets the nod in the hockey world.) Coons bought a plain, white, road hockey goalie mask with flexible straps at the back that wrapped all the way around his head. This wasn't a Jason, old school from the 1970s goalie mask; this thing was state-of-the-art, up-to-date road hockey technology. It looked like a real ice hockey goalie mask, and it lasted! Venkman even dressed it up by applying overlapping strips of masking tape all over the mask, so he could write on it. He drew a logo on the front and inscribed the words, "Protector of Mesh" on the back. The cover of this book is the mask Coons bought, and the artwork is Venkman's original design. After this mask, Joel brought in the less trendy, but still effective, Dominick Hasek-looking mask with a throat guard. I hated wearing the mask, and whenever

I played goal, I looked more like Lorne Chabot with a baseball cap on instead. Sure, I took a few in the face, but that's what makes us Canadian, right? Most of the time my face was numb from the cold anyways, so what's the difference? That white mask Coons bought soon led to Venkman getting a very stylish Patrick Roy designed mask. It was a road hockey mask made to look like St. Patrick's when he was in Montreal. Roy was the best goalie in the world back then, and Venkman was a big Canadiens fan, so it was a huge deal. Too bad that mask didn't last as long as the white mask. The Habs mask got chipped, broke and fell apart much like the Montreal Canadiens did themselves.

ONCE I GOT off the phone with everyone, I'd start getting things ready. Since Venkman lived just six houses down, he was always the first one of my friends out there. Also, since he was usually a goalie, he'd want to be out earlier to start gearing up. I'd begin by opening up the big, brown, two-car garage door at my house. Although it certainly was large enough to accommodate both cars, my parents had, only one was ever in there. The garage had a huge freezer, a massive black rain barrel, about fifty big silver cans of wheat, a workbench and tools. However, what took up most of the room was all of my road hockey stuff. I had at least one net, two sets of pads, blockers, trappers, gloves, coats, sweaters, jocks, hockey pants and no joke – about twenty hockey sticks. Each stick was at a different point of erosion.

Plastic road hockey blades lasted longer, but they sucked. Guys who used them were constantly bending them to keep a curve. Some guys would drastically over-curve their blades to the point where they resembled more of a lacrosse stick than a hockey stick. Since we had all experienced the frustration of plastic blades, wood sticks dominated. However, because wood blades wore down faster on asphalt, we all needed backups. A wood blade would get worn down to a couple of centimetres and still remain in the garage as Plan 'B.' Some who went through sticks more often than the rest of us (like Joel and Coons) had a few more twigs, but we all employed multiple options.

Another reason regular sticks propagated in my garage was because no one felt like taking their sticks home. Venkman would sometimes keep a net in his garage, but even he and Scott would leave their stuff at my house because everyone knew they'd be back tomorrow, so why carry something when you didn't have to? My parents probably weren't cool with it, but they actually never asked us to stop turning their garage into a locker room. We knew they parked one car inside the garage, so we tried to keep our stuff confined to one, fairly tidy area. However, with the amount of hockey stuff we had it was still a tight fit for the car to squeeze in there. The gear would go into a couple hockey bags against the wall and then get surrounded by the net(s) to maximize space. I don't know why, but most of us chose to use blue *Titan* hockey sticks. I remember them being cheap, so I'm going to guess that was probably the reason. You never know though. Jason Arnott may have endorsed them, and that could have been why too. (I used to watch this show called, *Be a Player* put on by the NHLPA. One time I saw Arnott demonstrating how to shoot a backhand and from that point on, some of us would call out, "Jason Arnott!" whenever we'd unleash a backhand shot. (Random story, I know.) So, we'd have all these Titan hockey sticks and the only way to tell the difference between them was by the way we taped our sticks. Venkman would spiral the tape all the way down the shaft. Joel would put a huge knob on the end of his stick. The Doctor, Fumie and Coons all used really long sticks while Beezer, Buff Dude and I, used shorter ones. Beezer and Buff Dude were short so it made sense, but even when I grew over six-feet tall, in grade eleven, I still used a tiny twig. I felt I could stick handle and get a better wrist shot with it. However, my slapshot was so ugly it was ooogaly. I would put just a little tape on the knob, just enough to know where to keep my hand, and that was it. Putting tape on the blade in road hockey was a big mistake. On ice, it helps grip the puck to your stick, but in road hockey the ball will stick to the tape, and you won't be able to carry it. You'd take a shot and the stick would go right over the ball. It was very frustrating and although we all put tape on our blades at one time, (probably because we saw the NHLers do it and figured that was the thing to do) we never did it again.

As I'm thinking about tape on the blade, it's funny how we thought we should or could do all these things just because we saw it on TV. Joel played ice hockey for five or six years. I played one year, and that was it. All of our hockey knowledge came from watching the pros and doing our best to copy them on the road. Using hockey tape was a good example of how ice hockey skills don't relate to road hockey. Watching the NHL, shooters made it look like they had so much time to glide into a shot or fake a blast. If you stopped moving your legs in road hockey, you'd stop, and you'd never get a shot off. In road hockey, everything happens on the go. Running and shooting at the same time can make accuracy very difficult. NHLers can stop and set up, or delay the action, using the large area to their advantage. Road hockey was always full tilt, especially when you played on a small surface like we did. Stopping wasn't something we did until someone scored, or the goalie covered things up.

One pro trick that did translate over to street hockey was faking the shot. You could get away with it maybe once a game, unless you were Coons. He was easily the strongest among us. I don't think Coons worked out, so maybe it was carrying all those newspapers and doing all the chores his step-dad made him do that built up his frame. If Coons was ready for a body check, you'd just bounce off him, and if he caught you off-guard, his checks would send you flying. With that strength, Coons could rip them, and he had a pretty quick wind up too. After his one year in goal, he played defence all the time. He'd stand at "the point" (we didn't have any lines painted on the road, but any place away from the immediate slot in front of the net was technically the point) and use his big, left-hand shot to drive the ball. The best you could do was try a sweeping point check because putting your body in front of his shot was madness. Some of the younger guys like Curly or The Beaver would take a Coons' slapper and go down in tears. Coons' shot was not only dangerously powerful, but it was also ridiculously unpredictable. He'd launch the ball all right, but a lot of the time it missed and we'd have to chase that freaking ball all the way down the street. I always hated when guys would miss the net. We tried to make it a rule that if you missed, you had to go get the wayward shot. However, not everyone followed that rule, including Coons. He was notorious for missing and not tracking his shot. I didn't have a bullet shot like Coons or Venkman, but I worked hard on my accuracy and made sure that I at least hit the net if nothing else.

WHILE I WAS getting the net out and finding my stick from the forest in the garage, I'd call on Scott and Pierre. I never learned their phone numbers because Scott wasn't a close friend and Pierre was an adult, so I never needed to talk to them outside of a game. Besides, it would've taken longer to find their numbers than it did for me to walk to their houses. Pierre was just a quick look in the driveway to determine his availability. He drove a red Honda, which pulled a trailer full of lawnmowers, trimmers, and hand tools behind it. Pierre owned a landscaping company, which Venkman, and I both worked for in the summer between grades ten and eleven. After that, I started working at the now, defunct White Rose while

Venkman stayed with Pierre for another summer. We knew that if that the red Honda was gone it meant that Pierre wasn't home and, therefore, couldn't play. It was possible that Pierre's son, Aaron, might have been home, but we only invited Aaron to play if Pierre came too. We all thought Aaron was too young to play, but Pierre was this cool forty-year-old who played hard and we had fun with him. I hope when I'm forty there'll be a group of kids like us that I can play road hockey with, the same way Pierre did. Scott wasn't out much, but if he was, he was usually at Curly's house. Curly didn't live far though, so that was never a problem. The issue was that when Curly wasn't in the mood to play, he'd take Scott down with him and then we would be minus two guys. Both were baseball guys first, but Scott was the stockier of the two, so he adapted to road hockey better than Curly did. Curly was one of the smaller players, and he tended to be an enormous suck. If someone got hurt, it was often him or if someone was going to complain about the cold or the conditions (like too many pebbles on the road), or blaming his latest fan on the thickness of his blade; Curly was the guy. Unfortunately, those two were joined at the hip, so you'd almost always get both. Having both play was great for numbers, but a drawback if Curly was on your team. Scott was a much better sport about things. He didn't complain. Even though he was younger than us, he made up for his age with his shot and defensive game.

CHAPTER 5
Facing Off

By this time, guys started showing up usually in the same order. As I said, Venkman lived so close, so he'd be the first to show up. Venkman would just walk into the garage and start putting the pads on, it was automatic for him. Secondly, I could see Coons coming from five hundred metres away. From bend to bend, Dante Crescent was a long street. The street led straight into a lengthy field. On the other side of the field was another residential street that was equally as long and straight. Although that was a few kilometres away, by the time Coons crossed the field, I could see him. It was quite a walk for him, but he was usually one of the first people to get there. Coons, Joel and Fumie all lived far enough away that they went to a different elementary school when the district lines changed in 1991, half way through grade seven. However, all of us – except Venkman – went to the same high school so maintaining our close friendships was easy. Even though Venkman went to the drug-infested (or so the rumour went) North Park, he still lived close enough that we could see each other every day, and so thankfully, our relationship never suffered. Coons had a bike ("The Passage Two"), but he usually walked. Even in the winter, he'd take the half-hour walk from his house to mine. Coons would wear this great, big, black and yellow Bruins coat with black sweatpants and even in the dimming light of a winter's evening; you could see him as he passed beneath the street lights. Whenever Coons got to my house, he'd usually be laughing about something. Coons had a great sense of humour and he and I had very similar tastes in movies. If he said it was good, I usually enjoyed it as well. Usually as he was walked up he'd be quoting something from a *Monty Python*, *Simpsons* or a Jim Carrey movie. Even now, after all these years, when I think of Coons, I can't help but think of *Ace Ventura.* That movie was hilarious, and Coons loved it! He'd be quoting from it all the time, "Allllllllllrighty then!" Nothing will ever replace the one line Coons forever cemented in all our memories. For a year in tenth grade, Coons quoted, "Ahhhh Ballet" from Simpsons, what seemed like every eight seconds. If there was a gap in conversation, he'd pipe up with his best Homer Simpson voice, and say "Ahhh ballet," followed by the accompanying "do, do, do's" heard in clown circus music. There was no question that, that was a funny moment in Simpsons' history, but man, he said that a lot. I must admit though; I'm laughing now thinking about Coons saying that line even though it's old and overused.

The gang from White Owl would be next, accompanied by The Doctor. Beezer lived a stone's throw away from

Buff's house, and so they'd always come together. Along the way, they'd pass The Doctor's house, so they'd pick him up on their way to my place. If The Beaver was playing, he'd also come with them. Sometimes, in very rare occasions, Kyle, Randy and Jeff would be part of the expedition as well. It was great to see two to six guys showing up at once, because even if it was just Coons, Venkman and I at this point, we'd have enough for a game, even if no one else showed up. White Owl was a pretty long walk. It was about a twenty-minute walk away from my house. So, sometimes the group would get a ride from Buff Dude's dad. Other times, Beezer and The Doctor would be walking, and Buff Dude would ride his bike. I don't know why he did that. It always sucked to ride when others were walking. You'd have to move so slowly that you'd be practically tiptoeing along. Buff didn't do too many stupid things; it was what he said that often caused our bewilderment. Buff said so many dumb things that we used to talk about writing a book filled with all his numb comments. I don't know if he was trying to be funny, or if he just didn't think before he spoke, but Buff Dude would say something with this big smirk on his face just waiting for a pop from us all, when the whole thing would blow up and someone – usually Coons or Beezer – would say, "Shut up Shawn!" Here's a classic from the Buff Dude commentary library:

"Is that twister the game or twister the movie?"

I don't even remember what the heck he was referring to, but he made sure we would not forget the line. I've been giving Buff Dude a hard time. He took all the jabs from us about his size and the things he said, but he was always there to play. He understood that we all got teased, but first and foremost we were all friends and nothing we said was meant to be derogatory. He was a real fun part of the group.

Playing sports, even recreational sports like our road hockey games provided competition, and when you have competition, you can get anger. Yes, we had our disagreements, our arguments and our hurt feelings, but they were infrequent and they never lasted long. I remember a time Venkman deliberately hit me in the nuts and while choking on my own balls in my throat, I ordered him to go home. The next day, however; when my boys had returned to their normal resting place, it was all water under the bridge, and we laughed about it. Forgiveness was a special quality that we shared among ourselves.

I can fit everything I know about Randy and Jeff in three lines. They lived next door to each other. I'm not sure, but I think Randy was at least a year older than most of us. He definitely had B.O., and he worshipped the ground Beezer walked on. Jeff was probably two years younger than most of us, and he was an annoying little insect.

Beezer, on the other hand, was the reason all of this was happening. We met in grade five on account of destiny. Initially, I sat on the other side of the room from him, but I wasn't doing very well in school, so the teacher moved me closer to his desk which happened to be behind Beezer's. I don't remember how, but at some point, Beezer introduced me to hockey. Before Beezer, I barely knew what hockey was. I was like an American. I knew it was a sport played on ice, and that was about it. However, I do remember quickly catching onto hockey and becoming extremely interested in it, thanks to Beezer's influence. It was funny because Joel and I had already been friends for a couple years, and he played hockey, but our friendship was strictly based on Transformers. I must've just been finally ready to embrace the game because in less than a year after Beezer and I met, I convinced my dad to sign me up to play ice hockey in the fall of 1989. I had never skated before, so I spent most of my time at practice with an assistant coach, learning how to skate. I probably had the puck on my stick for a total of eighteen seconds that year and amazingly, I wasn't the worst player on the team. Beezer never played ice hockey; in fact, he doesn't even know how to skate. But sometime before we met, he got into the game and taught me all about it. I can remember drawing hockey pictures with him in class. At that time, hockey was Beezer's favourite sport, and the Montreal Canadiens were his favourite team. Unfortunately, this rubbed off on me, and I was temporarily a Habs fan. We both liked Patrick Roy, but I couldn't have been a Canadiens fan for too long because I was definitely cheering for Calgary when the two met in 1989, Stanley Cup final. I would remain a Flames fan for the next ten years. It was interesting that Beezer, Venkman and I all placed Montreal as our favourite team at one point. Beezer influenced me and perhaps I influenced Venkman the same way. Fortunately, we all moved on at some point. Beezer followed his favourite player, Juri Kurri around for a bit, becoming a Kings fan then finally resting on Detroit in the late '90s. Venkman jumped the Habs boat to Vancouver when Pavel Bure began lighting it up. He's still a Canucklehead today.

Over the years, Beezer also experienced several different nicknames, including, Bran, Peanut (not my idea), B, Bees and at last, Beezer. As I mentioned, I was a small kid until seventeen. Buff Dude was always thin, but grew pretty tall after high school, but Beezer has always been the shortest one of us. Despite his lack of size, he was quick, and he had some tricks up his sleeve. Always a straight 'A' student, Beezer learned the game of road hockey and parlayed that into Gretzky-like numbers. Wayne put up four, two-hundred-point seasons in the NHL, and Beezer did the equivalent with us. Beezer set the season bench mark for us when he racked up 252 points in 25 games one season. Although *The Great One* is the league's all-time leading goal scorer, he's known for his assists (and rightfully so when you have more career assists than anyone else has points). Beezer was the same way. We would all keep track of our stats, game by game. (Beezer went the extra mile and did numbers for Randy, Jeff, Buff Dude, The Beave and Kyle too.) He still has those old stats' books. I can only hope to find mine buried in a box of my stuff at my parents' house.

We were the only group of road hockey players (of whom I'm aware) that actually recorded individual points. It sounds like too much work, but we would remember our goals, assists and points from game to game and from season to season, all the way across our "careers" in high school. I strongly remember adding up my career goals one day and realizing that I only needed one more goal to reach three hundred. It wasn't a good goal either. Not surprisingly, it was Beezer that set me up back door. Even with a yawning cage, Coons got a piece of it, and it just barely rolled in.

BY NOW VENKMAN, would have the goalie equipment on and would be eager to get moving. Sometimes we'd have to dig to find someone willing to play goal, but Venkman was always a given. He'd show up and just start getting ready. Venkman was always good in goal, but not limited to it. If Beezer was our Gretzky, then Venkman was our Mike Bossy. He had a hard, quick shot that resulted in a lot of goals when he decided to play out. I remember one "season" (meaning twenty-five games, so there would be more than one during a school year) when he played out most of the time (this was the year Coons played in net, giving Venkman the break to play out) he scored over sixty goals! However, most of the time, he was in goal and doing his familiar thing there. Road hockey nets are much smaller than regulation, ice hockey nets, and with Venkman's height, he would take up a lot of space in the butterfly. To make things more interesting back there, Venkman's thing was making sounds while he was in net. He'd let out a giant, "ARRRRGGGHHHH!" whenever he'd stretch or dive to make a save. Other times it would be sound effects like, "BOOOSH!" as he kicked a shot away. The most popular exclamation was Venkman's claim, "I got a piece of it!" If the shot was near the net, over the net or even in the net, Venkman would maintain that it didn't beat him cleanly. That shot could be over Zdeno Chara's head, and Venkman would let us know that he was the one who forced it away. Even though we knew he was exaggerating; we'd let him have his way most of the time.

Joel and Fumie would arrive at the same time. After Fumie moved, Joel would usually get a ride from his parents. I don't blame him because it was quite a hike, but with everyone else walking, it did make Joel look a little helpless. However, Joel was usually the other goalie, and he was always there (even if he was last), so I didn't care how he got there. The problem was (and it's not really a problem) Joel liked to talk. Whether it was about movies, video games, classes, his family or someone at school, Joel always had something to say. Which was fine, but he couldn't get into his goalie gear and talk at the same time. It would take him fifteen minutes to get the pads and everything else on. By then, the rest of us had been there for a while and were getting really anxious to start playing. I'd walk over to Joel as he was putting his equipment on, thinking my proximity to him would put some pressure on him to move faster, but it never did. He'd continue to talk about how to approach a girl, or what to talk to her about. I'd even try shooting on his net and only answering him half-heartily to hurry him up, but that wouldn't work either. Joel didn't care. All the signals in the world, whether verbal or nonverbal wouldn't make him shift gears. Coons would stroll over and say, "Joel, hurry the f*** up and get in net!" Joel didn't care. It makes me sound like a jerk for not paying close enough attention to my friend, but we were talking about wasting fifteen minutes of street hockey here! There would be plenty of time to chat about girls and other stuff at school. When the nets were out, road hockey was paramount.

Joel and hockey have been together forever. His dad was a big Bruins fan and Joel bought into it. The Bruins had some decent teams in the '80s and early '90s, so at least he didn't hitch his wagon to a lousy team like the Hartford Whalers or something. (For the first time in my life, I saw someone just last month wearing a Whalers' hat.) I can even remember Joel giving a speech about hockey in the third grade. The one year I played ice hockey; I played in the same league as him. He had always been a goalie, but by the time we were twelve he had outgrown his gear, and shots were beginning to frighten him. Again, I don't blame him because frozen rubber versus flesh equals deep contusions. I don't remember, but Joel tells me he recalls a time when our teams met on the ice, and I hit the pipe while he was in goal. Exasperated, Joel says he's glad I didn't score because I was terrible and to have that hanging over him forever would've been uncomfortable. I'll take his word for it because if it's true, that means I beat him, and he had to rely on his iron buddy to bail him out.

By the time Joel had arrived and started getting dressed, it would be after 10:00. We'd be bored with shooting on Venkman by then and/or Venkman would be tired of practicing, so we'd just sit and wait for Joel to finish getting dressed. Sometimes we'd go ahead and decide teams while we waited. This was always done by throwing sticks. For a few years, we had a lot of players to choose from. We had: Coons, Beezer, Joel, Venkman, Curly, Scott, Fumie, The Doctor, Randy, Jeff, Kyle and I, that meant five on five, plus a goalie. If we had this many, we'd push the nets further apart and play four on four with subs. To pick teams, everyone would put their sticks in the centre of the road. One of us would then get down on his hands and knees, shut his eyes and start mixing up the sticks. This person would then blindly throw the sticks from left to right until they were all gone, whichever side your stick landed on was your team. This method guaranteed that the teams were fair. Every so often, one side would get stacked, so we'd make a trade on the spot to even things out. Randy was a baby and would only play if he was on Beezer's team. Kyle was kind of like this too, but not nearly as bad. Even The Beaver, a twelve-year-old playing with high schoolers didn't care whose team he was on, in fact, he almost preferred it if he wasn't on his brother's team.

Once we organized our teams, Joel was usually ready, and we'd finally be able to begin. I would have been thinking about this since the last time we played (which was probably the night before) or at least since that morning watching highlights. Saturdays were special because we could play a few games without having to worry about diminishing light ruining our game. Beezer, Kyle, Randy, Curly, The Beaver and I always played forward, whereas Coons, Fumie, Scott, The Doctor and Jeff were always defencemen. Coons was quick and could carry the ball, so he was a rushing defencemen, but the rest of them pretty much stayed close to home. If Pierre was playing, he'd also play defence, and if Neal was playing, he'd only play goal. For some reason, I very rarely played with Beezer and Venkman on my team. We could play twenty-five games and for twenty of them we'd be on opposite sides. Usually, I'd be facing off against Beezer. Centre would be determined, and we'd place the ball there. The two centre men would line up, place their sticks on either side of the ball and raise them just over it, tapping sticks together at the pinnacle. After the tap, we'd place our sticks back on the ground beside the ball and repeat. We'd raise them three times saying, "N-H-L" and after the "L" we'd battle for possession.

I was always very aware of Coons when playing because he was a bulldozer out there. Coons could run fast, and he carried a long stick which made going wide on defenders easier for him. I never wanted to lose the draw and have Beezer deal it back to Coons. However, if The Doctor or Fumie was on my team, I'd feel a lot better. Fumie was the fastest and The Doctor was really good at blocking shots, so I felt better knowing that one of them could contain Coons. If I had Scott or Jeff back there then, it was trouble because it meant that I would have to be aggressive both ways. We never had offsides, but cherry picking was frowned upon. Thankfully, all the guys had the integrity to honour the code. I would always backcheck, but I wouldn't rush back and forth constantly. Since Venkman and I were often on opposite teams, Joel would most likely be my goalie. Joel was a good goalie. He even generated some creative things while in goal. He came up with using chalk for hash marks to remind him where he was in his net. If there was snow, he'd build a "Trickle Line." A trickle line was just a small lump of snow that stretched from post to post that would stop the ball if it was barely rolling into the net, and it worked. He also, on-purpose/accidentally would roll over and knock the net off, disallowing potential goals. Joel literally would say, "Tweet!" when he covered the ball to blow the play dead. We all adopted that rule, and I think if we all played tomorrow, we'd still use it. There would be no face-offs after the goalie covered it. The defending team was allowed to take the ball behind their own net and given five steamboats to make a play. After that count, the opposing team could pursue the ball carrier behind the net. With Joel goaltending, I felt good about covering the points and not the front of the net.

When it counted – like in high school track and field meets, – I was never a good runner. My lungs were glass, and I wasn't overly quick. I don't know why, I was always active. Aside from road hockey, I played a lot of pick-up basketball in my driveway with friends or my dad. Without the flat out speed to run through the game like Coons, Beezer, Venkman or Fumie had, I needed an alternative maxim. For any success, I had to rely on my stick handling, and shot to get me anywhere. I practiced those fundamentals all the time. When I couldn't play, I'd practice alone in the driveway. I'd get the net out and construct a "Mr. Goalie." Mr. Goalie was created out of all the goalie equipment I could find. I'd fill as much of the net as I could, leaving only limited areas to shoot and score. I'd lay the pads down on their sides, hang the blocker and trapper in the corners, put a garbage can in the middle of the net and place the goalie stick to one side. Using my imagination, I'd run around make-believe obstacles then fire on goal. I could do this by myself for hours at a time. It knew it worked because in a game I could get around guys and always I hit the net. I famously called my hockey stick, "The Wand" because of the magic I created with it. Years later, Buff Dude hung it on his wall like a trophy (with an included caption about its wizardry).

If we couldn't get enough guys to play a real game, then Venkman and I would play a game called five goals, ten saves. Venkman would be in goal, and I would have to score five goals to win, but if he stopped me ten times before I could, then he would win. These shots could be from anywhere, at any time. I'd start off on a breakaway, but rebounds were fair game. In all the years, we spent playing road hockey, Venkman, and I played five goals, ten saves, hundreds of times. We would often end our days with it, whether if it was just him and I out for a little shoot around or after a long Saturday of playing road hockey for ten hours. Five goals, ten saves was a staple between us. For nine years, Venkman prevailed in 99.9% of our matches. I won the last game we ever played when we were nineteen, and he was heading off to university the next day. Best of all, it's on film! His girlfriend at the time was generous enough to take pictures of this particular moment and although he claimed it was just another goal; we both know it was the historic marker. I guess Venkman would have to be a real jerk to deny it. I mean he won every other contest, so to lose one wasn't a big deal to him, but it sure was to me! The guys knew how special it was to me that they even made it the focal point of their wedding gift to my wife and I, many years later. On a sturdy piece of black mounting board, they blew up a copy of my big goal that measured close to four-square feet. They based their inscription on a popular credit card advertisement. It reads:

Used goalie pads – 80$

Titan hockey stick – 15$

Orange ball – 1$

Finally beating Paul in 5 goals, 10 saves on your 800th try...Priceless

Some of the personal notes written by the guys on there were also just as creative. Buff Dude wrote, "Thanks for letting me be there during the two biggest days of your life, today (wedding) and the one below (the goal)." Venkman penned, "Well Curt you finally did it, and it's on film!"

ALTHOUGH I PREFERED to cover the high man, I didn't mind getting in front of the net. However, if I did go down there, I knew who would be there waiting for me. Anytime there was a battle happening in the crease, it would be between Beezer and I. Later in high school, as I grew, and he didn't; there was quite a difference in size. Beezer was strong on his feet, so I had to basically fall onto him to get him to move. We never called penalties, so I'd be raking my stick up Beezer's spine and he'd stand fast. None of us wore hockey gloves, only winter gloves when it was cold, so we'd take slashes and hooks to the hands all the time. Every one of us had scars and huge calluses between our index finger, thumb and all over our palms. Our sticks would bear the battle scars of opposing sticks with off-colour rubs all the way up the shafts. You could easily tell who had been slashing your stick when someone used a different coloured shaft. While blue Titan's were our number one choice, other sticks did penetrate the mix and then it was even easier to notice contrasting yellow or red smudges on a blue base.

Seldom though did someone really get injured. The two injuries that come to mind involved His Royal Buffness. One was during a small game of two on two and one goalie in my driveway. This kind of event occurred when we couldn't field a full game. In this scenario, one guy would be the goalie and the others would play with one teammate and have to quickly change from offence to defence. If you were on defence, you'd try to keep the other team from scoring while attempting to get the ball past the end of the driveway. Once the one team successfully moved the ball onto the sidewalk, the two teams would convert roles. The goalie would have to remember who was doing what because his defence would be changing all the time and sometimes rapidly. In this particular game, Scott was my teammate, and he accidentally tripped Buff Dude as they were battling for the ball. Buff Dude fell on the edge of the landscape tie that divided the driveway and lawn. He immediately cried out the loudest curse I'd ever heard from him. "AHHHHHH SCOTT, YOU F-ING IDIOT, YOU BROKE MY F-ING HIP!" Buff Dude writhed around for a bit and was sore for about a week, but he ended up being just fine. He didn't actually break his hip or anything.

The second incident was an example of legendary sibling rivalry. Buff Dude and The Beaver were on opposite teams, and it was getting near the end of the night, so fatigue and temper may have been factors. The Beaver stole the ball off his brother, so Buff Dude responded by tomahawking his little bro over the back with a two-handed slash. We were stunned. The Beaver dropped and started crying, but his tears soon turned to rage. The Beaver got up and went right after Buff Dude. I can still remember it. The Beaver chased Buff Dude around the net while the rest of us watched in amusement. The look in Buff Dudes eyes was of genuine concern while, the look in The Beaver's eyes was pure revenge. Their rooms were side by side in their house. I wonder how Buff Dude slept that night?

Although I had the reputation of getting hurt the most, Joel was actually injured more than I was while playing road hockey. During his in-line days in 1996, Joel would keep the blades on for road hockey games too. For the only time in his life, it gave him a great speed advantage. Once while he was playing forward and I was in goal, I poked checked him and although I got the ball first, I got his skates second and he went down on top of the big goal stick. I never did see the evidence, but Joel complained for about a week about the "massive bruising" across both his upper thighs. Another time, Joel was playing out, and I don't know if he just didn't see the ball, or didn't react in time, but he stepped right on it and rolled his ankle. Joel went down like he was shot. Joel was a big fan of the movies. He could tell you anything about motion pictures. We used to have a great time making our own action flicks in the backyard with his camcorder. Later in high school film class, we were able to produce real, scripted, edited movies. Joel was very good at the technical side of filmmaking. He was our director, cameraman, editor, mixer, and producer. He just hated being on camera. So, I don't know if it was from all the movies he watched or what, but seeing him go down sure looked like acting to me. After a couple minutes, he seemed better, but when his mom came to pick him up, he limped like he was walking with a pegged leg. Incredibly, this wasn't the only time Joel stepped on a ball. While marching towards an empty net, Joel lost control of the ball, got it mixed up between his feet and biffed it. I think this was Coons' favourite road hockey story. Well, it certainly was in high school.

The biggest injury we had during a game was in grade eight when Venkman broke his arm. Again, I was in goal (I didn't go in net often, but obviously when I did, bad things happened) and Venkman was on his roller blades. There was a pile in front of my net, and somewhere in there, Venkman went down. It didn't look really bad until he stared up at me and said, "Curt, I think I broke my arm." I looked at his left arm, and his radius was caved in. I took off – in full equipment, pads and everything - for his house to tell his mom. When I got back, Venkman was still not showing any signs of pain, but he said, "Curt, man, I'm gunna puke!" He got kind of woozy, but he was fine. Venkman returned in a cast that covered from his knuckles up to his shoulder. As irony would have it, he was wearing a T-shirt that day which read, "Kick some Asphalt!" His mom was the first to sign his cast. She wrote, "You REALLY kicked some Asphalt!"

CHAPTER 6
A Dissident Is Here

Playing other teams was a real treat. We all liked playing among our friends; we got to know each other's strengths and weaknesses. However, as we got better, we really wanted to show what we could do. Playing Beal's team only happened a couple of times. It wasn't fair and thus, wasn't as much fun. Other than Venkman, we all went to the same high school and were pretty much always stayed together, so we didn't have much luck finding other people to play against. However, I had a friend from church that lived on the other side of the city and went to a different school. Rich was the funniest guy I knew. He came up with some real gems that turned into long-lasting idioms we still use today. One of them was his nickname. Rich had a younger brother, named Nate, and like most brothers, the older, one teased the younger one. Rich really knew how to annoy his brother. Nate's response was usually, "Shut up, Rich!" followed by Rich's outrageous laughter. Since Nate's voice was still changing, his hasty response would often sound shrill like, "Ut Rit!" It was fantastic! So, thanks to his brother, I started calling Rich, Rit.

Rit and I did a lot of dumb things together. We would go to the golf course late at night and race the golf carts across the ghostly summer hills. We would put stink bombs in people's mail boxes then knock on their doors and flee. If we weren't out goofing off, we were probably in his room playing pool and watching, *Tommy Boy*. Rit was always fun to be around. We lived too far away to walk or bike to the other's houses, so we really only saw each other at church or church activities. Rit was a good friend who liked hockey (not as much as I did), and he played road hockey a bit with his friends. I hung out with Rit's friends a few times and even played some road hockey with them. They were all good guys. The core of Rit's group included a chunky kid called Houlistan, a scrappy kid named Jay, and a redneck named Rick. Continuing the tradition, Rit, and I developed our own jargon, even for road hockey. We both loved the *Weezer* song: *My Name is Jonas*, so we decided to use some of their lyrics for code during play. Our code wasn't genius, but it was fun. If I wanted to set him up for a one-timer, I would say, "My name is Jonas!" which he would reply with, "My name is Wakefield!" Somehow the other guys figured this out (shocker), so it didn't work long, but we still liked the song.

By grade eleven, we had played so much road hockey that we became the best players we knew who didn't have any ice-hockey skills to lean on. It was not much of a complement, but it was something. Having played with Rit's friends, I thought it would be terrific to hook our teams up for a contest. On this particular day, I had a hard time finding players, so I had to employ Neal. We played three on three with a goalie against Rit's team. Physically, our team was much better. We played road hockey five or six days a week, while Rit's team played maybe once a week. In this game, it was Coons, Beezer, Buff, Neal and I against Rit's team. Houlistan was like Coons, but only chubbier. They were both perverts (and I mean that in a nice way, they'd never actually sexually harass a girl or anything). Jay was very quiet, conservative and thoughtful. Rick was unlike anyone I'd ever met. I never swore. Apparently Rick didn't either, so in lieu of that, he said "Frig," and he said it a lot! During our first match up with Rit's team, we played on an outdoor basketball court that was surrounded by fencing. This was great because we didn't have to chase the ball when it missed the net high or wide. The drawback was that the ball could roll under the fence and cause delays. As luck would have it, that ball rolled under the fence a million times that day! Every time it did, Rick said, "Oh Frig" in this quick, twangy-style that made it sound like it was all one word. "AHFRAH!" was what it sounded like. It was hilarious! All game long we'd be listening to "AHFRAH" and be laughing, but I don't think Rick knew we were laughing at him. The game was fun because we were playing against guys our own age and we demolished them. All of our skills were on full display. Coons was blastin' away; I was sniping and Beezer was dishing. We might as well have been playing Beal's team.

Now, Neal could be a good goalie. I don't know why he didn't play more, because he had this Dominick-Hasek-thing going that would frustrate the heck out of guys when he'd make these inhuman saves. However, his style could also let him down. He has allowed some brutal goals. We never knew which Neal would show up. This wasn't a game by game thing; it was a shot by shot thing. He could literally take away a goal one minute then give one to you the next. One time, Neal made an outstanding glove-save on Fumie while he was staring at an open net. Fumie screamed, "F*******K!" as loud as anyone could yell. It was the first time any of us had ever heard him swear. Then again, I saw Neal let in rollers that were so slow you could read the label on the ball as it passed by. Thankfully, on the day against Rit's team, Neal was pretty good. The only shots that got by him were deflections off his own teammates. Rit's team only played us once more after that. After losing for the second time, I think they realized they didn't have much of a chance, so they turned us down for a third game. Another reason was probably age. While most people stopped playing actual road hockey on the street by their high school sophomore or junior years (I'm not talking about professionally organized tournaments because they still draw men of all ages) we kept playing until the gang had to break up after high school ended. Even in our final year of high school, when we all had part-time jobs, dates, even the odd girlfriend, we'd still find time for road hockey. Whereas most other, older teens (like Rit's team), gave up on the road hockey games by grade twelve to concentrate more on girls or whatever else occupied their minds and time.

Girls were certainly part of the equation, but Beezer was the only one who consistently had a girlfriend. The rest of us concentrated on what we were good at, and that was playing road hockey. In grade ten, Beezer even retired from road hockey to be with his girlfriend at the time. That was a tough year. We lost Beezer and, with Venkman at another school, we didn't have his influence around us all the time. Beezer started hanging out with this big kid named James. We all had known James since the seventh grade. He and his friends were more into basketball and football, so I think that it was because of them Beezer started to enjoy these sports more than hockey. If you ask me, this was a gross error in judgement. Right up until then, Beezer was still was our good buddy. He played road hockey with us all the time, but he started to play other sports too. Basketball was OK. Venkman and I both played in my driveway, club ball and on the school team. However, starting in grade ten, we hardly ever saw Beezer. He had his first steady girlfriend, named Carlana (a fusion of her parents' names – clever). She was very attractive. I think I only met her once or twice during the several months they dated though because Beezer started to hang out with her and James' crowd more than he did with ours. James was a real tool to most people, including Joel, Buff and I.

He'd put on this obedient, pretty boy act for teachers and parents, but he was a real mean kid. He was bigger than all of us, but he wasn't someone who would beat you up. He just had a smart mouth and a pile of friends he would use to intimidate and humiliate you. We never talked to James. He thought he was better than everyone else. He was very condescending. I suppose Beezer got along with him because they both loved football. Beyond that, I can't image why Beezer would associate with such a cruel human being.

Given their new bond, Beezer always wanted to invite James to play with us. Consequently, all of James' gang wanted to play too. None of them were hockey guys. It felt like an infection having agreed to allow these invaders to play with us. I didn't like James or his friends, but road hockey ruled, and I would have played with the scum of the earth if it meant regular, well-attended games.

With an influx of new players, someone came up with the idea that we should develop a new way to organize/pick teams. It was suggested that instead of throwing sticks and having new teams every time, we form four permanent teams. We created balanced schedules, standings and of course, scoring leaders. With so many people playing each night, we actually needed two games going on at once. One game occurred in front of my house while the other took place down the street in front of Venkman's. The top four scorers from the past season would "draft" the other players. We then had a season with team records, playoffs and the whole shebang. We also introduced full body contact for the first time during this experiment. We allowed body checking for years, but only in the snow, so if someone fell, it wouldn't hurt as much, but now it was an open season. I had a bad feeling about this from the start, and I didn't help myself out either.

Beezer had won the previous scoring crown and chose to select Kyle first overall. The provision to such an unusual selection was Kyle's cousin. Apparently, his cousin played junior hockey and wanted to join our road hockey league (how he was going to do that and play junior at the same time never occurred to us). Naturally, this unnamed superstar would only play on his cousin's team. It was a little dirty, but there wasn't much we could do to stop it. I certainly wasn't bold enough to tell anyone I felt they were cheating. I had finished second in scoring, so I used my first draft pick to select Joel. I'll defend my choice because Joel was a multi-faceted road hockey player. Joel was a very good goalie as well as a strong forward. Coons finished third and drafted Fumie. Venkman was forth and picked Buff Dude.

Before the first game of our new system, I made a colossal blunder when I traded Joel to Coons' team for a guy named Jason. Jason was a new player, although he was not part of James' entourage. I had never seen him play road hockey before, but I knew he was a really fast runner and a pretty strong guy from his history as a cadet. Even though we were only acquaintances, I traded for him anyways.

Jason had an unfortunate nickname that had followed him for years. Back in grade five, he spilled something on his shirt (that looked like puke), so the kids started calling him, "Barf." Despite how long it lasted, Jason never complained about it. I think it finally ran its course by the time he graduated high school.

Anyways, my team consisted of Jason, myself, and my second and third picks (Scott and Curly). We discovered early on that we were the worst team in the league. To make matters worse, Jason got caught stealing two candy bars from *Zehrs* and his parents grounded him for a year and actually stuck to it! So, basically my blockbuster deal lasted two games. Then I was down to just three players. None of the other guys could even join my team because they were already with someone else.

There were bigger problems with this new format that went deeper than poor trades, rigid teams and schedules. This league format created unnecessary aggression too. It went further than just full body contact. At first, checking was kind of cool. It made us feel like big shots to slam into each other all the time. Obviously you can't generate the speed in road hockey you can in ice hockey, but we were still hitting each other pretty hard. Especially since none of us wore equipment. Our stick was our only offensive and defensive tool. However, the hitting didn't last. The smaller guys couldn't participate in it, and it became just a flavour of the week, dying out of practice quickly.

It was the new guys who were ruining our games. With no hockey skills, James and his pals couldn't actually play, so they used intimidation. Their language and physical strength really turned many of us into church mice, playing conservative, zero fun, street hockey. Coons was the only one who was as physically strong and as verbally abusive as James' group. Because of that, they left him alone, but they were merciless to Joel, Buff, myself and even the younger guys like Scott, Curly and The Beaver. The entertainment was being suffocated. Road hockey became a job you hated going to, but you continued to go to do it because it paid well.

I was in a bad place. I hated the new format. I traded away my best player and now, worst of all, my favourite activity was being devalued. I was obsessed with road hockey, and I didn't appreciate it being negatively altered. Beezer didn't care as much. James was a tool, and his friends were uninterested, careless monsters...and now they had sticks!

My watered-down team was like Kool-Aid without sugar. It wasn't good...not even a little a bit, and it was now too late to change the flavour. Teams just played down to our level and would enjoy a couple subs while we burned out after thirty minutes. Another problem with my team was our goaltending situation. I could play goal (not well), but I was our best scoring threat, so I always played out. Curly was a pansy so that left Scott. He didn't mind playing goal, but he was far worse than I was. We got spanked every game and in fact were even shut out once. It was the only time in street hockey history that one team was shut out. I'll never forget it.

We were playing Coons' team (Coons, Fumie and Joel), that game. Coons was good. Joel was a solid, reliable player and even better goalie, but Fumie was so impossible to get around, it was stupid. I think Coons felt bad for us, and put Fumie in net that game, even though Fumie had never played one second of goal in his life. Our only good scoring chance came when I had a partial break, but Coons was faster than me, and he was catching up. I had to hurry the shot, and as Fumie went down, he got just enough of it to deflect the ball over the net. I can still see that orange ball softly floating over the bar, and behind the cage. I didn't even get a chance at the rebound. Since Curly was useless, I was pretty much doing everything all game long. Scott would be lucky to stop it (he was too afraid to go down, so pretty much anything along the ground with speed would beat him) and Curly had so little finish that I couldn't even count on him to cherry pick. I was running back and forth and most of the time, too late to help since Coons figured out he could just wind up and blast it in. Using his speed, he'd avoid my harassment, and get close enough to the net, so his chances of missing were slim. We didn't win a single game all season (0-25).

Thankfully, it only lasted one season, and it was all over before we finished our first semester. James showed up every game, but the rest of his core friends only came out to one or two games. Once they discovered that road hockey wasn't their thing, they quit. It was a pain playing with those guys. They didn't really care about road hockey; they just wanted to feed their egos and display their ignorance. James would show up halfway through a game and at the end, claim he registered fifteen points. It was impossible, yet he maintained he did it. This coming from a dude who showed up to play road hockey in Doc Martins and khakis. After the season, James felt he was too good for us and left to pursue his regular narcissistic endeavors. Glory, glory halleluiah! All of us realized that the new league system had serious flaws, and so we went back to normal after that. Kyle's cousin never played a single game, and I never did find out if that dude really played junior or not. He would've been a dynamite junior player too if he was playing at that level when he was only fifteen to sixteen years old.

For the rest of the year, we never saw Beezer. Sadly, his long reign as scoring champ ended. He just stopped playing after James quit. In one small regard, it worked out well for me. I captured the point crown that year, but my numbers never approached Beezer's. It wasn't a good trade. I would have preferred that Beezer stayed and kept dwarfing my numbers than him leave (and lose his friendship) and be the lead scorer. It was strange not having him around while we played road hockey. It was even stranger not hanging out with him at school. Beezer and I had been friends for five years by that point, and I didn't want to see the friendship end. It's very strange to witness a relationship slip backward, especially when it happens so quickly. In a matter of a few months, Beezer went from our close, road hockey friend to a guy who didn't care about us or road hockey. No one in our group had changed, it was Beezer that changed, but why he began to reject us was something I never figured out. Did he view the rest of us as immature simpletons? Did he just begin to believe he had more in common with James and his group than he had with ours? Personally, I felt Beezer started to believe road hockey was for kids and was embarrassed to still be playing it in grade ten. I never once felt I was too old to play road hockey.

Beezers defection made us all very sad. We missed him. He was a leader, a competitor, and he was good company. He was not just my good friend; he was all of ours. He was gone with no warning. It was as if a ninja had kidnapped our friend during the night. For months, Beezer didn't treat us like he used to. The longer he stayed away from us and road hockey, the more hostile he treated us. Friendly conversation had been replaced by polite nodding of acknowledgement to total disinterest. We continued to invite him out to play, but our invites were rejected. We didn't want to believe it was over, but there was a period where it was over. For about eight months, Beezer had removed himself from the group, and it appeared he had moved on.

The rest of us kept playing street hockey. We went back to the traditional method, using random teams and familiar stipulations. There were three periods, first team to five goals won the period; then we'd switch ends. The game was over when one team reached fifteen. Most of the time, the games were long enough to last a couple hours. During the winter, it would be nearly dark when we started and completely dark by the time we ended. A lot of the time the games were close too. I can remember someone calling, "next goal wins" and getting that big time feeling like I was about to hit a walk off home run. I can remember two game winners; one where I was the hero and one where I was the goat. The latter is more entertaining so I'll get to that one second.

Both situations came on White Owl. I don't know if it was this way or not, but White Owl seemed to have better street lights. Maybe there were more of them there. I had a pretty good game this time. My shot was on, and I was finding the holes. I already had a few goals this game and scoring on Joel wasn't always easy. Joel was a pretty big guy and with his history of ice hockey goaltending he knew what to do in there. This particular "overtime" (tied at fourteen) was going longer than most. I was feeling confident when I got the ball on the sidewalk. It was a point of sportsmanship that only one person would get the ball on the sidewalk or if it went onto someone's lawn. So, I had the ball in an uncontested area and decided to take a moment to check out the scene. Most people gathered in front, of the net, one might be at the point, and one way back in a defensive role. Joel was hugging the post, and Beezer was four-feet away from me on the road. I trusted my shot and let her go from twenty-five feet away. This particular shot had some mustard on it, and the ball zipped past Joel, low on the short side. I really put that thing in a shoe-box. Joel fell back in his net and lost it! He was so mad, he started throwing his gloves and taking his anger out on the net ah la Ron Hextall. I can still see that ball going in. I was careful to only engage in modest celebration afterwards because to whoop it up in front of an angered Joel would have been a bad decision. He was already feeling bad enough without me rubbing it in. Not a good goal, but it was a good shot.

The next time I was in goal. Every now and then, I honestly felt like playing net, but sometimes no one else would, so I strapped 'em on just to get the game going before things got too late. I know I wasn't good, and although I watched a lot of hockey and thought I knew the game well, I couldn't put any of that TV knowledge into a game. My glove was atrocious! Any shot between my elbows and the crossbar had a strong chance of going in. Although my foot work was decent, I could get deaked out quite often when coming out to use my size in an attempt to cut down the angle.

For some reason, on this night we were using a tennis ball. We'd lose hockey balls all the time, and there were always more tennis balls around than orange balls. Most of the time, we'd lose the orange balls in the dark, and find them later. However, sometimes they'd roll down a sewer or Coons or Joel would miss the net by a country mile, and it would go over a fence, into some bushes or some other forbidden location. At this particular time, the play was at the other end of the road and I was left to my own thoughts. I noticed Venkman golf one out of his zone and toward me. For some reason, I decide to come way out and try to catch it. I wasn't being hurried, so I don't know why I did this. Anyways, I lumbered out, then changed my mind and realized I wasn't going to make it out in time to catch the ball. The ball hit the ground right in front of me, and I went down on one knee. Maybe it was an old tennis ball, or maybe it was the compact snow beneath us, but that ball bounced up high, over my head and landed without a roll into the net. Game over. That was the closest I got to experience how Doug Harvey felt in overtime of the seventh game during the '54 Stanley Cup finals. Detroit forward, Tony Leswick, dumped a high shot into the Montreal zone before going off on a line change. Harvey raised his hand to catch the puck, but it tipped off his all-star hands, down the shoulder of goalie Gerry McNeil, in the net, and the Red Wings won the Stanley Cup. Coons told me after that he had a feeling the Hail Mary was going in. He said the whole thing just looked awkward from the start. At least I was able to laugh about it shortly afterwards, I don't think Harvey ever laughed his off.

CHAPTER 7
Who's Goin' In?

There was always a debate about who the better goalie was: Joel or Venkman. I'll tell you one thing; Venkman will always get my vote just because he always seemed to have my number. Five goals, ten saves was one thing, but Venkman had the ability to come up with these stunning saves that really got into my head. I think both were good, but for me, I could score on Joel, whereas it took a lot for me to beat Venkman. Maybe it was because we played so much when it was just the two of us that he really got to know my ways. I was always a shooter first and liked to think I could beat most goalies with a good, hard wrister. However, Venkman must have known that and he used his cat-like reflexes to stay equal to my shot. I can remember sitting at home or playing in my driveway, specifically thinking of new moves just so I could use them to score on Venkman. I knew I could score on him because he never shut me out in five goals, ten saves, but during a game; it was rare for me to beat him with a wrister. I'd have to try to screen him and jam one by him in tight. I can remember Venkman stealing many away from me even in this situation. He was just naturally quick. We were practically the same build, but he was born athletic and blessed with good reflexes. His glove was the source of many nightmares for me. Sometimes he really did, "get a piece of it," but if I were the one shooting it, he'd catch that thing. He'd make it look easy. I think Venkman stepped up when it was me shooting. Perhaps he knew we had a fun rivalry, and he enjoyed stopping me more than the other guys. I can remember feeling more joy scoring on Venkman than any of the other guys.

Comparatively, scoring on Joel was a little easier. It was probably all a mental thing, but I can remember scoring on Joel from the seat of my pants whereas that never occurred against Venkman. Joel was thicker than Venkman and about the same height, meaning he took up a little more net, but physical appearance wasn't the key distinction between them. While Venkman was all about reflexes, Joel was positioning. He knew where he was supposed to be and focus on anticipating the next shot. Joel could analyze the last shot for hours and often he would. After each goal, we'd get a commentary on how that one beat him. Joel would say stuff like, "If I just moved my glove another five degrees down, I would've had it." Joel's critiques were pragmatic, "I saw you look like you were going glove-side, so I was ready." They weren't unworthy analyses; they were just unusual. Who says stuff like that?! That was Joel though; he was a thorough dude. Most of the time, we didn't care. We liked to tease him about how detailed he was. That quality helped him make some really fun movies, do well in school and create conversation topics, but it didn't carry the same weight with us during our games. Joel's comments were better received in the post-game.

Venkman and Joel also had very different personalities. Venkman was very easygoing while Joel, on the other hand, was much more intense. Venkman had a very laid back attitude. He was calm about anything he did. Playing forward, playing goal, big games, school work, tests, even at his job, he was always level. I'd describe him as confident but not overbearing. Venkman liked to have fun and road hockey was fun and challenging for him, so he kept playing. Venkman smiled all the time and loved nothing more than to rob you. Remember when Roy stole one from Tomas Sandstrom in the 1993 Cup finals and winked at the Finn as he skated by afterwards? That was Venkman all the time. You could see him smiling through the mask and then get a slow-motion, instant re-enactment of the theft. Joel certainly loved to play as well, but he just didn't display it as often as Venkman. Joel didn't smile or laugh as much during the game. He was far more focused than Venkman. I think Joel was trying to keep up with his goaltending counterpart and needed the tunnel vision to help him do as well as he wanted to. When things didn't go as planned, Joel could really go off the rails. I've seen Joel lose control and start throwing things out of rage. If he didn't like a goal, he could go anywhere from, copious amounts of vulgarity to net dismemberment to total disintegration of the goal stick. I've seen all three more than enough to pull out a few memories.

First the swearing. Joel, with a face distorted with anger, would vehemently utter his worst and most popular phrase, "I'm gonna punch you right in the f***ing head!" Let the record state that he never did. Secondly, he was also capable of taking his frustration out on inanimate objects, not just people. Our hockey nets were just constructed out of hollow plastic which probably weighed just fifteen pounds. Joel would sometimes swing his right arm and clock the post with his blocker. Or, he would shove the cross bar. Either action would send the net flying and cause the joints to fall apart. I don't think Joel ever broke a net with his tantrums, but it was annoying to have to chase down all the parts and put them back together. The last act is a popular action among hockey players at almost any level. Breaking your stick is the easiest way to let everyone know you're not in a good mood. Although I've never broken one, I'm sure a goalie stick is harder to break than a regular stick, just because of its size and thickness. Joel could bust a stick with fantastic form. One time he bashed a stick for a bit then tossed it like a Frisbee. I was standing on the sidelines and took my eye off Joel for the one second he launched the wooden missile. Next thing I knew, that stick smoked me right in the head. Fortunately, it was the handle, not the big paddle part that hit me. Still, I went down. To show my displeasure, I confiscated the lumber and made Joel play without the stick until he cooled off. Thankfully, no matter how angry he became,

Joel always calmed down pretty quickly afterwards. By the end of the game, whatever bothered him was ancient history. Too bad he couldn't have gotten over things just a moment faster to avoid the freak-out. Only once do I remember Venkman spazzing out, and it was quite a different experience. I don't remember what he was mad about, but without any expression on his face, Venkman (almost calmly) went over to the net and slashed the post in half with his stick. At least it was his net and not mine. He fixed it later by using the shaft of an old stick to fill in as the new post.

If there was a stick-swinging champion though, Coons was the winner hands down. Since Coons always had a job, either a paper route or at *Wal-Mart*, he always had money, and he liked to spend it. Coons went out for lunch every day. In grade ten, it was this fish and chip place. He'd order the same thing, day in and day out. In grade twelve, he went to *Timmies* every day before school. With all this money, he was able to replace all the sticks he shattered. One time, his step-dad took him down to Buffalo for a *Sabres* game, and somehow during the game, his step-dad stole Donald Audette's stick and some hockey tape from the Sabres' bench. So, Coons showed up the following day for a game with this big grin on his face bragging about his new stick. Audette was a decent player then, not a superstar, but using a Donald Audette stick was still pretty cool. Plus, he had the daring story to go with it. However, the stick probably would have lasted longer in the hands of its rightful owner. Late in the first game, while using the

Audette stick, Coons had a good scoring opportunity but missed the net. Coons went into a rage and repeatedly smashed his stick against a lamp post, destroying the stick in seconds. I don't know why he was so upset; Coons missed the net all the time.

The best stick-smashing incident happened at one of our street hockey tournaments. From grade eight to grade twelve, we entered our team into real, professionally organized, road hockey tournaments. One year, we played in a tough engagement that went into overtime. Joel was in goal, and he was lights out! Even with some of his strongest goaltending, we still fell 3-2 in the extra period. Normally Joel would freak out on the net, but he was too exhausted and just laid there. Coons, however; was a little more animated. After shaking hands with the victors, Venkman approached Coons and said to him, "Where's your stick?" Coons responded by pointing in various directions and saying, "Over there and over there. There's some there..." In his disappointment, Coons had shredded his stick and tossed the remnants into the wind.

The drop in goaltending quality was dramatic after Joel and Venkman. Neal would play, but he'd only play about once a week and that was a good week. Coons only played goal one year and almost never again. Beezer and I were laughable in our feeble attempts to stop the ball, so we only ever went in goal out of dire need or because we felt like goofing off. Same with the Doctor, but he played a little more regularly than Beezer or I, but his quality of goaltending wasn't much better. Guys like Kyle, Jeff, The Beave, Randy and Curly never played in net. Those guys would rather not play at all then play net.

If we needed someone, we could usually count on His Royal Buffness to go in. He was like our third stringer, but that's not giving him enough credit. Buff wasn't too bad at all. He was quick, but his size hindered him more than anything. I'll tell you one thing; Buff was creative. He had his own little highlight feature he used to call the "S.A.M," an acronym for Shawn A. Move. This dandy piece of work is an exaggerated glove-save on an easy shot. Buff would take anything, even slow-rolling shots; scoop them up with the big mitt, and thrown his left arm up and over his head like he had just snagged wild game. It was a classic Patrick Roy or Mike Palmateer (depending on your generation) move. It always garnered our attention when he'd whip that little specialty out of his goaltending quiver.

Buff could crouch like a cat. He was a small dude most of those years, and he looked like Terry Sawchuk in there with such a low centre of gravity. The old ice hockey pads the taller guys like Venkman and Joel used were too high for Buff so when he'd go in net, he'd wear these tiny foam road hockey pads. They were no more than a thick layer of ordinary foam buried in a heavy, grey nylon exterior. He was the only one small enough and light enough to use them. The foam worked better than it looked like it would. Buff never got hurt going down on the road or when taking a shot. The only problem

Buff Dude had in goal was his dreaded five-hole. Being as small as he was, and with such a poised, low approach, you'd think he wouldn't have much of a fivey, but boy did he ever! His five-hole was like the German Autobahn... stuff went through it, often and in a hurry. If Buff only let in five goals all game, each one of them would've been through that five-hole of his. He could stop shots with the blocker, trapper and his body, but the lower half of the net was where you could beat him and everyone knew it. I especially tortured Buff's fivey. I would score so frequently on him in that one area that it became a joke. It got to the point where I could be moving in on Buff Dude and say, out loud, "Buff, I'm going to shoot it through your five-hole," and then proceed to do so. I don't know if he thought I was playing mind games or if my shot was just that good (I'm pretty sure it was the latter), but that five-hole was money in the bank.

*Coons (blue sweater) feathers one back door to Joel
(red sweater) as Beezer (goalie) tries to intercept.
Check out all the duct tape on Beezer's pads.*

*Buff Dude preparing to test
Venkman on a breakaway.*

*A view of Dante from where one net
would sit, right in front of my house.*

*Beezer and I await the balls arrival in front of
The Doctor (note the ball glove and ski mitt).*

Celebrating the good times! I finally beat Venkman in five goals, ten saves. Buff Dude witnesses in the background. Poor Venkman (or any of our goalies) had to layer up with sweaters to tend goal whenever we would play in the summer.

A look of the road from White Owl where one of the nets would be placed.

*Buff Dude (5) and Joel (8) both hunt for
the rebound, while Venkman (goalie)
keeps his eye on the loose ball.*

*The Brantford Black Bears inaugural appearance
prior to our first three on three tournament
during the spring of 1993. From left to right we
have: Fumie, Venkman, Coons, myself and Joel.
We were outscored 19-3 in our brief debut.*

The Brantford Black Bears make their second trip to the annual three on three road hockey tournament in 1994. From left to right our team is: Sandy, myself, Coons, Joel and Venkman. While our offence improved from the year before, our defense gave up nearly 10 goals a game during our three contest trip.

The Brantwood Park tennis/basketball court where we first played, "The Church Boys" and later on, the Brantford Fear from time to time.

Joel fires a slapper on Beezer as Vanderwoude tries to deflect it. Look at the road, it had more ice than a skating rink! We didn't care because we'd play road hockey during any type of weather conditions.

Long after high school ended, we'd still get the gang together for a game of road hockey when we could. From left to right: myself, Beezer, The Doctor, Joel, Buff Dude, Coons and Venkman. This picture was taken during the summer of 2003.

Spending a whole day playing road hockey was the best way to spend a Saturday. We would easily put in a nine hour day of playing. Left to right: myself, Beezer, Buff Dude and Venkman.

CHAPTER 8
Participation Ribbons and the Infinite Sadness

Road hockey tournaments were very exciting to prepare for because they were real competition! They were what we imagined playing in The Stanley Cup Playoffs must have felt like. I loved playing with and against the guys on the street – it was all I wanted to do - but every spring we felt a particular exhilaration as we geared up for tournaments. Tournaments offered us a change in scenery, diverse competition, real wins and losses, and they served as a measuring stick for us. I have great memories of these events, from fabulous take-offs, to crash landings.

Buff Dude started the tradition in grade eight (1992) when he got some flyer with Brian Hayward on it promoting a three on three tournament. Brain Hayward was no Patrick Roy, but he was his backup, and that was pretty cool. He also had the best mask in the NHL while playing for San Jose. His mask had sharks teeth all around it, some even dripping with blood. The tournament was a two-game elimination system with each game consisting of one twenty-minute period. You were guaranteed two games, and if you lost both, you were out. There were several tournaments organized all over southern Ontario, but we chose to enter the event in Kitchener because it was the closest to us.

It was a great setup in the Kitchener arena. They took the regulation-sized rink and divided it into thirds with boards, real nets, referees, and scoreboards. I remember seeing the hard, smooth concrete surface for the first time and thinking how incredible it was going to be to play on such a nice place. We didn't have to worry about bouncing balls, tripping over rocks or stalling for passing cars. Buff enlisted a friend of his we didn't know, along with Beezer and I. We thought we would do pretty well. The tournament setup was literally three on three; you could only have three people from your team on the floor at once, instead, of three players and a goalie on the floor. We decided to play three out in our first game with one of us just playing stay-at-home defence. The plan failed; we didn't stop much from going into the yawning cage. I remember thinking before the game that we had Beezer, Mr. Art Ross, so there was a good chance he would lead us to victory or at least a close game. I don't want to pin this all on Beezer because it certainly wasn't all him; I didn't play well either. It was just that Beezer didn't light it up in the tournament like he did on Dante or White Owl. Twenty minutes into our first tournament appearance and we were 0-1.

We were one game away from an early exit, so we decided we better try using a goalie this time. Our decision meant that Buff Dude got the nod to play between the pipes for game two. To put it mildly, the move didn't work out. Buff Dude was REALLY small back then. His diminutive size compared to a real, four-foot by six-foot net - not the shrunken, road hockey nets we always used – meant that opposing shooters saw plenty of mesh behind him. Much to our disappointment, our new strategy failed. With only two guys playing out, we couldn't generate enough offence, and Buff Dude was getting beaten like he stole something. We got bounced hard and fast from that first tournament, only scoring just a couple goals in the whole process. Sadly, it would be five years before Beezer participated in another tournament and Buff's friend never played road hockey with us ever again.

Right off the hop, in the '92 tournament, we were doomed because of our name. Buff Dude went ahead and called us, "Black Lightning" without asking anyone of us for our input. That needed to be changed, but more than ever, I just wanted to show up and not get creamed. I waited impatiently for Bryan Hayward's tournament to return. We decided to go back to Kitchener the next year. Thankfully, they made one change that drastically improved the tournament that year. Instead of three on three including a goalie, they got it right and went with three on three plus a goalie. This time we had Coons, and he had been a rookie sensation with us. In his first-year playing road hockey, Coons was always a goalie; he was like Ed Belfour back there. It was quite rare for a rookie 'tender to dominate, but Coons was the exception.

We all shared a desire to be anything but, "Black Lightning" and Coons had big influence on our new team name. Coons was born in Maine, and it was the University of Maine Black Bears that inspired our team name. In the 1991-92 college season, The Black Bears – lead by Paul Kayria – went 42-1-2. Coons reminded us about it all the time! That's how I still remember it all these years later. It was an inspiring story and with Coons' persuasion, we all went along with it and called ourselves the Brantford Black Bears from then on. We even created our own logo. It was a giant black and blue "B." We drew and coloured our names and numbers on the back of generic, white T-shirts and wore them to the tournament. Armed with a new name, a year of preparation, new rules, and sharp new uniforms, we felt indestructible going in.

New look aside; we had a better team in 1993. Coons was a good goalie, and we also went with our top goal-scorer, Venkman out front. With Coons in net, Venkman got to play forward for most of the year; he was like his favourite player Pavel Bure out there. Joel and I provided a two-way sense and Fumie was our rock, solid D-man. I had previous experience at the last tournament, and knew how everything worked, so I was the captain.

We went with those rubber, Cooper road hockey pads that gave out huge, unpredictable rebounds. I thought they would be good here because we could use the boards to gather up those rebounds and turn the play around. That strategy didn't work. We played a team that had one dynamite player on it, and we couldn't stop him. This guy single-handily beat us. None of us were nearly as good as we thought we were. We were all just running around, chasing the ball in an unorganized way. We had no strategy. Usually, Fumie was such a dynamo on defence but here he wasn't. Maybe it was the different setup or the larger arena that affected Fumie's game. Or, perhaps this tournament just exposed Fumie's lack of hockey knowledge. Like I said before, Fumie was a fantastic athlete, but he didn't have much experience with the game. Maybe he was upset at himself for drilling Coons in the chest during warm-up, and that was bothering him. Fumie could really hammer it, and Coons wasn't wearing any upper-body protection. My dad taped the game for us, and you could see Coons buckle over from the pain when he got hit.

The special player they had was getting all kinds of shots. Although Coons stopped a few really good chances, and the pads did indeed kick out rebounds, the playing surface was too small, so the shots that hit the pads often went soaring into the adjacent rink, stopping play. There was no doubt that the playing surface was a factor here too. We trained on rocky asphalt. So, we were used to the speed of play on asphalt. Unfortunately, the slick, smooth surface resulted in a much faster game. One we were not prepared for. We lost our first game 6-0; four or five of the goals were scored by that one guy.

The mood was not good heading into our second contest. Coons was unhappy with the team's performance and made sure to tell us that during the first game. Whenever we had a moment's peace in our own end, Coons would yell at us, "Score a friggin' goal!" Obviously, we were trying, but I can understand his frustration. Even with the best goaltending, without goal support the best you can hope for is a tie. In our second game, we changed the way we played. We noticed that the other goalie was only wearing shin pads instead of goalie pads. So, I asked Venkman to cherry pick while one of us stayed at centre or high in the defensive zone, and the third played deep in the defensive area. This plan might have worked against the last team we played, but this second team was just plain better than us, so there was no strategy that would have resulted in a win against them. We were all fifteen at the time, and I'd estimate our opponents were about eighteen.

The new strategy did have some of the desired effect though. We played much better in front of Coons, and we even scored a few goals. Venkman got our first goal of the tournament by scoring on a breakaway. I blocked a shot, (which left a HUGE contusion on my calf) and then sprung him. I don't know if he slipped, or if he was showboating, but Venkman lost his footing, and while falling, he buried it. It was a sweet goal, and it's on tape. Unfortunately, we stayed at one goal for a bit while the other team kept scoring. With the game far out of reach, Venkman sniped his second with a good, clean wrist-shot while he was alone in the slot. Then

Joel got a real beauty to cap off our scoring. I took a long slapshot that hit the goalie up high, rebounding off the glass behind him. With some of the best hand-eye coordination I'd ever seen, Joel picked the falling ball out of mid-air, and swatted in it. We got drummed 13-3, but at least two of our goals were good-looking ones. I finished with two assists and two massive bruises on my right calf that were perfectly round and just bigger than the orange ball. They were like tattoos! This was the last time for years that Coons would play in net. Sadly, our second tournament was over in a hurry, just like our first one.

Tournament number three (1994) was a little different. We went into the Hamilton tournament this time, and we had to change one member of our team. Fumie moved to Connecticut after grade ten, and we never saw him again. He and I wrote a few times, but it lasted less than a year. It was too bad because he was a great guy. He scored 100% in most of his classes, but he wasn't a nerd. Fumie was really funny and was in tip-top shape. We all enjoyed his company. Coons took over as captain and became a very strict but rewarding leader. He took everything very seriously. He reminded us to keep our toenails trimmed, and he made us practice drills and memorize the plays. Coons wanted everyone to know their role and to train for it. He specifically picked on me, at first I didn't know why. I was always a good player, and I did have a decent second game in '93. Regardless, Coons said I needed to add the one-timer to my skills. At the time, I didn't understand why because I worked on my wrist-shot all the time, and it was good. I felt the one-timer was for guys who couldn't pick their spots, and relied on speed more than accuracy to score. To me, the one-timer was an excuse for players who didn't have the ability to snipe. Coons would spend the first twenty minutes of practice with me, developing my one-timer. I was really bad at them. He could put it right in my wheelhouse, and I'd heel it, fan or just miss the net. I can still remember being very embarrassed about having to work on this portion of my game. I remember being even more ashamed that I wasn't doing very well at it. Coons tried to teach me using - what he called -"constructive criticism," but I felt he was just nagging me. I understood the need to run more and improve our cardio, even trimming toenails regularly was something strange, but I went along with it. The one-timers though were something I didn't tolerate well. Coons and I would always fight about their necessity. It turned out that Coons was right and after weeks, my one-timer was good enough to use in our games. I used it often with success.

We remained the Brantford Black Bears and added my cousin Sandy to the team. Sandy was good at road hockey, and we played together a lot that year. When I would go to his house in Hamilton, we'd play, and he'd do the same when he came to Brantford. All my friends got to know Sandy pretty well and aside from Joel; they liked him. Sandy was a good finisher, and I often set him up, so we called ourselves, "The Cousin Connection." However, Sandy was also just a road hockey player like us, he also had zero ice hockey experience. By this time, we were sixteen-years-old, and the talent level at the tournaments was increasing. That was something we didn't pay any attention to though. We didn't concern ourselves with the obvious dichotomy between ice hockey experience and no ice hockey experience. Road hockey was a different game, and no one played more than us. We felt that would replace any recessions. We worked hard to be ready for this tournament and we all had the group experience at these events to win now.

This was around the time when Beezer had left our group and was being poisoned by James and his nonsense. Even though Beezer wasn't really playing any road hockey with us, he was offended when I didn't include him on the team. He became really sarcastic and would constantly "Thank" me for the lack of invitation. I would be eating my lunch in the hallway, and Beezer would deliberately walk right on both of my ankles, squishing them under his feet. This was always followed by a disdainful "Thanks." It was one of the strangest trials I went through in high school. To experience a very close friend, turn rapidly into an antagonist was mind-boggling. Especially, when I never did anything wrong or different. Beezer shifted priorities and drifted to other activities. He wasn't driven away by us or anything we did. For a time, Beezer was nowhere near the road hockey gang and his attitude towards us encroached hatred. The only explanation I have for this is James. James hated us, so by extension; Beezer despised us too.

Venkman went in goal for this one, and he had everything he needed. He even wore our best equipment. I felt with Venkman back there; he'd maybe even steal the game for us. However, we found out that tournaments were not Venkman's specialty. During our games on Dante and White Owl, he was the best goalie among us, but in tournaments, he never put on the same kind of show. He always said he felt fine, and that nerves didn't affect him, but he looked different in tournaments. He appeared slower; he didn't have his usual swagger.

We provided Venkman with good goal support in our first game of that year's tournament. In the first ten minutes, we scored five goals and led by that margin halfway home. Although we had practiced the specific positions for months, we quickly got away from it. We were supposed to be playing the same way we did at home. Coons on D, Joel in the middle, and "The Cousin Connection" up front. Of course, we couldn't employ this at all times because we could only have three guys on the floor at once. For the first couple of minutes, we stuck with it, but as soon as we made our first line change, the system broke down. I don't know if it was because I played well on defence in '93, but all of a sudden I switched and played stay-at-home defence. Oh well, it worked, and the addition of Sandy was paying off too. My cousin scored two of our goals and made it look easy. Our effort was finally paying off, and we felt confident.

However, the other team started to get rough, using cross-checks, elbows and slashes to get some space.

Penalties were called in the tournament, but instead of two minutes for an infraction, the victimized team got a penalty shot. Like my dad had done the year before, Coons' parents taped this tournament as well, and you can see in the video that there were several blatant attacks on us where the ref chose to turn his head. Their strategy worked because we started backing off, and they started scoring goals. The last ten minutes went from a dream to a nightmare; they came all the way back to beat us 6-5. It was a horrible loss. We were all so frustrated with the lack of sportsmanship and the blind-eye officiating. We knew we had played well enough to win, and so that was even more frustrating. So, instead of celebrating our first ever tournament win, we were again, facing elimination going into game two.

Venkman decided he'd had enough and pulled the plug after this one. Between games he said, "I'm not playing net anymore." I seriously thought he was joking. Venkman was a goofy guy. He would do strange things like play a game on his knees or play so far out of his net he looked like a defencemen masquerading as a goalie, so I didn't believe him right away. However, after he repeated himself a few times, I realized he was not kidding around. The obvious choice to play goal after Venkman quit was Joel since he was our other regular goalie. However, he played very well as a forward in the first game, and so he declined. Coons was our goalie the year before, but he hadn't played in net since then, and he said there was no way he was going in. Besides, Coons was probably our best player in the first game, so we needed him out there. Sandy had never played goal and so he didn't want anything to do with it either. Like Coons, Sandy was providing the offence, and we needed him to continue doing that. That left me to don the pads and work the net. I played goal every now and then, but I wasn't very good. I guess since I was the only guy who didn't score in the first game, and was playing strictly defence, I seemed like our best (only) bet.

I can remember warming up before that second game, and feeling pretty good. I knew I wasn't great, so my expectations were pretty low. I felt that if I could just make some key saves, we'd be all right. I never expected to steal the game, and the guys knew that. I can remember debating in my mind whether or not I should try hard during warm-up. On one hand, I thought that if I tried too hard, I might use up all my luck before the game. On the other hand, I thought that if I didn't try, then maybe I could fool the other team into thinking I wasn't very good (which was true, but they didn't know that). I decided I needed all the fortune I could get and went with option two. I took the warm-up very casually and deliberately created the impression that practising meant little to me. I was hoping our opponents would see this and believe I didn't care because I didn't need to try in the warm-up. Perhaps not a great strategy, but I was doing this for the first time, and it was all - at best - educated guessing.

The game started out well. I was seeing shots pretty clearly, basically I just used the butterfly position and went down on everything. The guys knew they had to be a little more aware, so they didn't give up any real good chances for a while. I remember being fine until the first goal, and then I wasn't the same. It was 3-0 before we got one; Venkman drilled it home. Venkman had such a quick wind-up, and he just blasted it. He was doing what he came out of the net to do, but it wasn't enough. We suffered from several missed calls in the first game and ironically were caught twice in the second game for infractions. On the first penalty shot, Coons came to me before the whistle and whispered, "Poke check him." I nodded, but instead of being patient for an opportunity to use the poke, I went right after the guy and dove out towards the ball. I missed, and the guy easily cashed in. The second penalty shot was the exact same thing. I went out, missed and was helpless. The final score was 9-4. On the bright side, we produced more offence than ever before. Venkman and Joel each had a pair in the loss. Joel now had three goals in two games. Despite how exciting that was, the depression from losing another tournament trumped that. I never played in goal during a tournament again.

As we trucked our slouching, collective girth out of the rink, we received some unexpected and delightful news. There were some teams that failed to show, and so the tournament organizers had to shuffle the format on the fly. This resulted in a bonus, third game for us. However, we were told that if we lost this one, we were done. For the first time in an organized tournament, we played outside the arena. Since the tournaments were becoming more, and more popular using just an arena was no longer sufficient to accommodate all the teams. To solve this, pop-up rinks were built in the parking lot. We were so excited! We totally thought we had an advantage because we were back on the asphalt. Venkman went back in net, and I went back to defence. Also, for the first time, we met our opponents before the game. They were a real nice bunch of guys which was a treat especially considering the guys we met in our first game that day. Each tournament was played for money, so it was not exactly accurate to call them recreational, but this team certainly made us feel like we were back at home, playing on the streets.

Despite being loose for this one, we played our worst game of the entire tournament. The players on the team were nice all right, but they were way better than us. They basically couldn't twitch without scoring on us. I can't confirm it, but they must've all been junior 'A' players. Coons did have a real, nice end-to-end rush that resulted in a sweet goal and even better sound bite though. After his spectacular goal, Coons' mom shouted, "Yeah!" in a very cute, high-pitched voice. It was like a single mouse squeaking in an empty auditorium. We all found that hilariously entertaining. We listened to it over and over again on the video recorder. Too bad it was the only good highlight of the game. After already receiving one penalty for unsportsmanlike conduct (which they scored on), Coons got another one in fabulous form. One guy fired a long, hard slapshot from way back in his own zone, probably forty feet away from Venkman. I tried to block it, but instead of actually getting in front of the shot, I just stuck my leg out and the ball hit the top of my foot tipped up and over Venkman's arm and into the net. To say Coons lost it would be an understatement. In perhaps the most awesome display of anger I've ever seen (even to this day), Coons raised his stick over his head and drove it into the ground so hard that the stick's splinters exploded all over the playing surface. He continued until there was nothing left to swing. The referee gave him another unsportsmanlike penalty and a game misconduct. They scored on the resulting penalty shot and beat us 12-2. Joel got his fourth goal of the tournament during that game. He was not only our best, but most consistent player that weekend. Coons played well, but his penalties lead to three goals, off-setting the three he scored. Sandy didn't score after the first game, and I certainly had my worst tournament ever. I didn't record any points and was responsible for giving up almost a couple touchdowns.

We didn't enter the Brian Hayward tournament in 1995. I don't know what the tournament was called, but I remember Brian Hayward wasn't part of it anymore. Instead, we hitched our wagon to a local tournament. It was nice to stay in Brantford, but it was a larger, four on four structure. A nice feature to this tournament was the use of bench players. Earlier tournaments only allowed five guys on a team, but now we could sign up almost twice that amount. We recruited just about everyone we knew for this one. Joel, Venkman, Coons and I were all there, plus we also leaned on Buff Dude, Venkman's friend Gary, Curly, and The Doctor. Even Beezer was scheduled to make his long overdue return.

Having left our group and road hockey behind during the start of second semester in 1995, we had all gone several months without Beezer's friendship. However, by the fall of grade eleven, he and I started to become good friends again when we sat across from each other in math class. I was terrible at math and required a lot of one-on-one support from the teacher just to get a sixty-five. I think Beezer took pity on me because of my ineptitude. He must have pitied me or else why would he have turned down his girlfriend to work with me on a major assignment. I remember him telling her, "I better work with him or he'll fail." Beezer was dating this very nice girl named Katy. Katy was down to earth and so I think dating her helped humble Beezer. After a few months, we started to hang out again. When winter came around, Beezer decided to give road hockey another go. He didn't enjoy the game the way he used to, nor did he play as much, but I appreciated having him as a friend again anyways.

Gary was a guy who had played with us a few times before this tournament. He was a good guy who liked to play goal, and that was fine with us. As it turned out, Gary and Joel were teammates years before during pee-wee ice hockey. Based on his willingness and our need, we even put Gary in for the first game of the Brantford tournament. We liked the idea of Gary in goal because then we could use Venkman and Joel up front. We knew

Venkman could score, and Joel was our lead scorer in the previous tournaments, so we needed him on offence too. Ironically, if Gary played well, we wouldn't need either of our top goalies to go in net.

The Black Bears were hit with some bad news just days before the tournament though. Beezer had come down with mono, and we couldn't find anyone to fill his position. Thankfully, we were still able to dress enough guys to participate, but we were short on subs. Although not our first choices, we had to ask The Beaver and Curly to step up. The Beaver had demonstrated his ability to score on Dante and White Owl while Curly was just there because we needed bodies. It sure was strange showing up to this road hockey tournament full of sixteen- to eighteen-year-olds with a couple of tweens.

Our plan failed to materialize when Gary's goaltending fell apart in our first game. I shouldn't have been surprised, but I was. We put a dude in net whom we barely knew! The most vital position to any team's success and we went with a big, fat question mark. He didn't stop much, but our top guys didn't help much either. We got ripped 8-2. One of our only goal-scorers was The Beaver. Like I said earlier, this little guy knew how to score, but he was so much younger and smaller than us that he was really a boy playing against men. To think that this scrawny little thirteen-year-old was playing with a bunch of seventeen-year-olds was actually quite impressive. I remember his goal coming from the tough spot too, right in front of the net, and shovelling home a rebound. That kid showed a lot of bravery going out there. As a whole though, our team lacked chemistry and structure, and it showed. We were everywhere and nowhere at the same time. I think it was the greater number of players and larger playing area that caused our bewilderment. Rarely did we play four on four. Also, it was only during tournaments that we'd play with boards, and that alone created an entirely different dimension. We weren't playing as a team; everyone was playing an individual game. Unfortunately, we didn't have enough talent to win on pure skill against the team we were playing in our first contest. We needed to make some changes.

The second game; however, was perhaps the most enjoyable game we ever played under the name Brantford Black Bears. We made a goaltending change and called Joel's number to keep us alive. Despite being a regular goalie for us, this was the first time Joel 'tended during a street hockey tournament. He was brilliant in there. This was where Joel cemented his name as a money goalie. While Venkman struggled in goal during past tournaments, he was still regarded as the top goalie during regular street hockey games. However, from this moment on, Joel was viewed as the best guy in goal when it counted. The team we played was very similar to ours. We could tell they were not a bunch of ice hockey players, trying to pound our inexperience. Like us, they were just a group of friends who played regular road hockey and that's the only skill they had. It was a close contest with the teams trading goals until it was tied at two. Joel had played well up to this point, but it was his save in the final minutes that I'll never forget.

The opposition had this one Native American guy that was very muscular and fast. He was probably a running back for his high school football team. Given the space he could create with his size and speed, it was amazing he didn't score at will. With the clock winding down, I remember him getting the ball and just taking off. I was in hot pursuit but could not stop him. He was a right-hand shot, and he moved with such speed that Joel couldn't back up as quickly as he would have been able to most other times. This guy deaked to his right and looked like he had Joel beat to the glove-side, but Joel dove back, reaching with full extension to lay the glove down and take away a sure goal. I can still see how he did it! It was perhaps the biggest save I ever saw. It was certainly the save of the tournament. Moments later, Venkman received a penalty for slashing, but in this tournament, the player sat off for two minutes instead of giving up a penalty shot. While shorthanded, I managed to steal the ball as the D-men played catch at the line. I was all alone with time on my side. I never liked to deak much because there was always the possibility of losing the ball, and besides, I trusted my shot. So, I ran down the left-wing and from 10-feet out, zipped a wrister into the far-side top corner. I didn't stop to shoot and just kept running after scoring. I ran back to centre in celebration. That shorty proved to be the winner in a 3-2 Black Bears win. Our first win ever!

Our joy was dimmed by news of our next opponent. Playing a team full of Midget "AAA" players we knew from school left us feeling like we had very little chance of winning a second game. These guys played us hard too. They were constantly checking us into the boards and were really pushing on our smaller players. And man, could these guys move the ball around! They looked like a bunch of all-stars with their passing, shooting and play development. If any of us managed to get the ball, the best we could do was scoop it out of there. Thank heavens for Joel because he was the story again. The shots must have been a 15:1 ratio. We were so outplayed it was a joke, but Joel wasn't giving them anything and you could see it was affecting them. I remember talking to one of their players when we were both on the sidelines and saying, "Are you going to stop toying with us and score already?" He replied, "We're trying! Your goalie is stopping everything we can throw at him." Eventually, Joel wore down and gave up a couple goals. We lost 4-1, but it should've been much worse, if not for Joel's heroics. No one can ever take away what Joel did that day. For all the saves Venkman made on me during our lives, and for all the games I watched him win playing on Dante and White Owl, none of that came close to what Joel showed everyone that day. Joel's performance here was the best any of us had ever seen.

Our last high school entry into a road hockey tournament was in grade twelve. It was an outdoor tournament again, but this time it was in London. It was a five on five format. The playing surface was much larger than we had ever used before as well. This was the tournament we exited on the bad line change in overtime when Coons broke his stick all over the place (refer back to chapter 7). It was all the guys: Buff Dude, Coons, Venkman, Beezer, Joel, The Doctor and I. We also used Beezer's sister's boyfriend and his brother, both of whom played ice hockey. We left the smaller guys like The Beaver, Scott and Curly at home. The previous years' experience showed us how unlikely it was that those guys would enjoy playing and how little they could contribute. Joel was an easy choice in net. We even redesigned our T-shirts and logo for this one. Joel and I both took photography in school that year and we learned how to make iron-on prints. We had Jason (same kid who briefly played for us and stole the candy bars) design a new logo for us. Jason was a good artist, so we had him draw an angry black bear in a hockey helmet clawing at a big "B." It looked really good and over the next couple of classes, Joel and I printed the logo on all nine T-shirts.

I remember not enjoying this tournament as much as the others. The outdoor rink was so large that I felt lost out there, and even though I was fit, I became dog-tired after only a few minutes. Skating a regulation-sized rink is so much easier than running it. Trying to run back and forth across a rink is like shoveling snow with one hand. It's exhausting (even when you're fit) and hard on the body. However, the organizers wanted it to be authentic, so they decided to use a two hundred by eighty-five-foot playing surface. It was a rainy day in

London too, so it was much cooler than a usual day in May in southern Ontario.

Aside from Joel's marvelous goaltending, very little went right for us in this tournament. Venkman was the only regular to score that day. The rest of our offence came from the new guys. We didn't know them very well, but Beezer said they were good guys, so we took his word for it. They played hockey better than us that was for sure. I remember one of them firing a slapshot and it was the fastest thing I'd ever seen! To my astonishment, the opposing goalie caught it too! I thought it was Patrick Roy in there. Before seeing these guys play, I believed my shot was good, but it was a whiffleball compared to theirs. Too bad neither of these new guys seemed to care though; they just kind of drifted until something offensive came their way. It was clear that Beezer was right about their abilities, but they didn't mesh with the rest of us. We didn't act or play our usual way. I know I certainly didn't. The dynamics of the team were off. Either we couldn't keep up with their skill level or we just didn't know how they played because we never even practiced with them before. It was a mistake to invite the new guys. I think we did it because we wanted to win so badly. However, by doing so, we tampered what we enjoyed about playing. Looking back it was very selfish of us to do that, especially in our last tournament together.

In keeping with tradition, we lost the first game as a part of our now sacred strategy to fall instantly behind. Luckily, the second game was an improvement.

I even had two great scoring opportunities during it. Unfortunately, I flubbed them both. The first was early in the contest when Venkman set me up with a lovely cross-crease pass between the defenders, but was stymied by the goalie. Had I one-timed it, I would've scored, but instead I stopped it and attempted to flip it upstairs. My delay allowed the defenceman to slash my stick, and I didn't raise the shot enough to get it over the goalie. My second chance was a real disaster. As we nursed a late, one-goal lead, I caused a turnover in our zone and broke out the other way. Normally, I would have gone to the net and tried to generate a scoring play. I don't know if I was nervous or what, but instead I chose to simply kill time and dumped a slow-roller, around the boards and behind their net. One hundred times out of one hundred, the carrier should create something and to pass on such a wonderful chance displayed just how far off my game I was. Even a poor shot on goal would've been better. It turned out to be an even more regretful decision than I could have ever dreamed.

Although my offensive instincts were not sharp, we did get some offence to lead 2-0. With Joel's incredible, unwavering performance behind us, it looked like we might hang on and win. However, as everyone should know, you can't just hang on in hockey and expect to win. Our opponents attacked us relentlessly and cut the lead down to one. We began to hold our sticks a little tighter. The pressure was terrible, and it wasn't fun. I was so nervous. I just wanted the game to end. Regrettably, we didn't push back enough, and they tied it. I felt so bad for Joel because he was competing so hard, and we weren't reciprocating. Joel was the only reason the game went into OT.

Overtime was a terrible place to be. I didn't want to start. I wanted to watch things unfold and then, hopefully, contribute. Overtime started when regulation time ended and Joel kept kicking 'em out. Starting on the bench in OT, allowed me to really appreciate the excellent work Joel was doing in there. After a couple of minutes, I was chomping at the bit to get back into the game and was calling for a line change. As I watched them storm our zone, I heard Beezer calling my name to sub on. I couldn't believe it; he was changing it up during defensive zone pressure. He hoped off, and I quickly jumped on, but it was too late. They scored before I could even get into the play. Sadly, we lost 3-2. I was crushed; we all were. Gaining a five-goal lead in the '94 tournament only to lose sucked. Giving up ten goals in a single game was brutal, but this defeat really stung. I felt like someone just ripped my heart out.

If we scored even a few more goals we might have won a game, or possibly two because of Joel's sparkling net-minding. Once again, he did everything humanly possible to steal those games, but we let another super goaltending performance go to waste. It was too bad we didn't win more tournament games. We always tried so hard, and we always talked about how we could get better, but all the preparation we went through and all the planning couldn't make up for our lack of hockey

IQ. Guys who play ice hockey get coaching, instructions, format, live and meaningful pressure situations not to mention tremendous shooting and play-making abilities. No amount of road hockey could bridge the gap between our collective talents and those who augment road hockey with ice hockey. We only knew what worked on Dante and White Owl. Even though we got better each year, it never showed in the results of these tournaments.

CHAPTER 9
Road Rivalries

When we weren't playing in organized tournaments, we were trying to put together our own little events. We didn't play Beal's and Rit's teams enough to call them rivals, but later in high school we developed rivalries with other teams whose talent, and experience was closer to our own. In grade eleven, I met a guy named Richard. I worked with his friend Koptie in film class. Richard, Koptie, their friend Bill, along with Beezer, Joel, The Doctor and I created a movie called, "Terrorists Attack PJ." (Pauline Johnson was the name of our high school, but it was always referred to as PJ.) It was a huge, high school hit. Film teachers used it to show future classes how to make movies. After school, we were allowed to run around the halls with cap guns acting out violent scenes. This sort of thing would not fly nowadays. I wouldn't say we were crazy. We were just seventeen-year-old boys and what teenage boy doesn't like action films filled with brutality? Anyway, we all became friends because of the project and continued to work together on new movies too. We found out that their group of friends also enjoyed road hockey and played a lot themselves. This was perfect! Guys we knew, who were nice guys that seemed to be just like us. Most of them went to the same church, so Coons decided they would be called, "The Church Boys." We immediately set up a game with them on our turf.

The Church Boys didn't like to play on the street, so we found a tennis/basketball court close by (on Brantwood Park Road) and played there. It was always a treat to play in an enclosed area. We had gotten used to the luxuries of playing with boards and fences around us because of all the tournaments over the years. We still played up to fifteen and would cram in as many games as we could in the allotted time. I missed our first game against The Church Boys because I had to work and couldn't get the time off. The realities of growing up were finally catching up to me. However, I was very excited to hear the game report at school the next day. It was just what I had hoped for. The Black Bears had won the match, and everyone had a good time because both teams played fairly. After creaming them in our own backyard, they wanted another crack at us, but they wanted home, "road" advantage this time. We were happy to oblige them.

The Church Boys had a different definition of street hockey than we did. We actually played on the road. We stopped and moved for passing cars, ran onto neighbour's driveways, shot the ball into people's gardens, and kept our heads up to avoid running into street lights. These guys had a looser interpretation. They never actually played on the road. For the first time ever, we rented a gym and played in there. As we discovered, a gym was a great place to play. It wasn't much bigger than the area we usually competed on, and it had walls to keep the ball in play. Plus, it came with regulation-sized nets. Playing in the gym made us feel like we were big time now. Since we all found it to be the best use of space and execution, we always played three on three with a goalie whenever we met The Church Boys.

They chose this location because they considered it their home advantage. They all preferred playing in a gym over playing on the street; they only played in a controlled environment. We always tried to find as many guys as we could since we had to split the cost of the rented gym. Our new member, Gambicourt, made his Brantford Black Bears debut in the gym. Gambicourt was a computer geek who was voted most likely to succeed after graduation. He was a nice guy, but he was only ever a school friend. We rarely spent any time with him outside of PJ. Gambicourt slowly became more accepted into our group, and by our senior year (in 1997), we honoured him with another classic chain of impressive nicknames. It went from Gambicourt to Gamby, to Lockport Gambino, (The name of a car dealership in Western New York. Some of the TV we watched was broadcasted out of Buffalo and commercials for *Lockport Gambino Ford* played all the time.) to finally just Lockport. He was not an athletic dude, but he really wanted to play, so we let him.

Probably the last time I played floor hockey in a gym before The Church Boys was during intramurals. I remember using those flimsy plastic sticks and the soft rubber puck. Hockey was always fun, but this was the least fun way to play. I loved hockey so much that I suffered through the frustration of whipping fans and rolling pucks just to play. I can remember stepping into this old gym - on the other side of the city - that had to be at least fifty-years-old. Despite living in Brantford most of my life, I had never been to this part of the city. The gym was dimly lit compared to other gyms I'd seen, but that didn't matter because low light was never enough to stop us.

After stomping on The Church Boys in our first meeting, they let us have it the second time – well, at least in the beginning. We quickly fell behind 2-0 before The Doctor buried a rare goal. From then on, it was all Black Bears. As a stay-at-home D-man, it was very rare to see The Doctor in front of the opposition's goal, but there he was, slipping home a rebound. The Doctor was the Ken Daneyko of our team. He could play defence, but we didn't count on him for rushes or scoring chances. Fascinatingly, he surprised us again that game by scoring a second goal to tie it! Using his off-speed slapper, The Doctor managed to record his first, two-goal game ever. His offensive outburst inspired us, and we unloaded on The Church Boys. I enjoyed a statistical feast during this set. I pumped in goals and loved every minute of it. Even when my shot didn't go in, someone was there to clean up the garbage, and I'd pick up an assist. We played a couple games in the three hours we had the gym for, and we won by a landslide in both. Even Lockport scored! He came rushing back to the sidelines with such enthusiasm after his goal that his high-five he toasted me with almost ripped my arm off! The Church Boys were really good about it. Even though we could see their frustration, they never resorted to stick work or anything chippy.

Since we all liked the gym so much, we decided to just keep playing there, rather than going back to the street. We didn't call on Scott, Curly, Beave or anyone else when we played the Church Boys. Venkman, Joel, Coons, Beezer, Buff-Dude, The Doctor and I were all we needed. Boy, it was fun playing them! It was everything we wanted in a game. They provided good, fair competition. We always had even numbers. Plus, there were no equipment advantages or ice hockey experience to tilt the floor in either direction. When we played these guys, it was great because they were our friends, so even when we'd beat them by a mile, there were no hard feelings. Perhaps it was our years of tournament experience, or maybe just the total number of hours we spent playing, but we could always top The Church Boys. Our goalies were better, our instincts were sharper, and our shooting abilities were a level ahead of theirs. For a guy like me who loved to use the wrist-shot and was used to firing on road hockey nets all the time, my eyes lit up whenever I got close to those big four-foot by six-foot cages. Excessive amounts of twine looking back at me made me giddy. I would simply pick a spot and cash in. I loved it! Scoring goals was always fun, but dumping in rebounds or tipping in shots wasn't as rewarding - to me - as a good, clean wrister, beating the goalie.

What was really exciting was when I got to combine school work and hockey. If there was ever a chance for me to gel the two together; I happily took advantage of it. It didn't happen too often, other than in media classes though. We made road hockey highlight videos featuring new music, our own Black Bear logo, T-shirts and more. Using our photography skills, Joel and I, made our own hockey cards based on the series we had with The Church Boys. On the back of my card it read: "5GP, 8G, 11A & 19PTS." I wrote, "The Magnificent One was a scoring-machine this past year, leading his team in both goals and points." Beezer edged me out for the lead in assists by two helpers. I put that homemade card in a top loader and kept it protected with all my NHL cards.

As we entered our final year of high school, in the fall of 1996, we all had part-time jobs, so finding a time when all of us were available - including The Church Boys - was hard. Sometimes it would take weeks to coordinate a time to play. I was working at *White Rose*, Beezer was at *McDonald's*, Joel, and Venkman were at *Wendy's*, Coons worked at *Wal-Mart*, The Doctor was at

Cashway and Buff was at *Zehrs*. However, even though we were all busy, we still made time for hockey. We played as much and as often as we could. Sadly, after a few more games, The Church Boys decided to stop playing with us. After losing so many games, I think they just didn't find it fun anymore. This was sad though because we really liked those guys. Playing them felt like a good balance between competition and sportsmanship. I wish we met earlier in high school, so we could have played them more often.

We had a fun rivalry with The Church Boys. However, without question, our biggest rival was The Brantford Fear. We played them for years and definitely more than any other road hockey team. I don't like to say it, but The Fear were a bunch of guys we knew who were the misfits of the school. Ryan and Allen were considered the biggest losers at PJ. Ryan had a learning disability and got teased a lot for many years. I felt bad for him and never teased him myself, but I never stepped up and helped him either. Ryan, if you're reading this, I'm sorry. His younger brother Allen saw what was happening to Ryan and tried to rebel and become a bad boy. He put on a tough exterior, but he really was a decent guy. Then there were the twin towers, Donny and Dave. One of them was a couple of years older than us, and the other one was a year younger than us. Both were unpleasant, tough, nasty kids. When they played, a couple of our guys got the "Flin Flon Flu" so to speak. We came out to play, but didn't play our best in the face of these two intimidating forces.

The captain of The Fear was Sean; he was a decent guy who had a talent for organizing games. Like us, Sean and his friends wanted to play all the time, and they also made a team logo. Using the same helmet, and the masking-tape method Venkman used on our mask, Sean drew and painted this psycho-looking clown on his. It was a good piece of artwork, and the clown really did represent fear. Sean and Coons shared a few classes together from 1995-1997 and became the team representatives; they would work together to arrange the times and places of the games. Sometimes they'd come to Dante and sometimes we'd go to Ryan's street. Other times, we'd play at the basketball court on Brantwood.

We never developed a relationship with The Fear outside of playing road hockey. To us, they were just the opposition, and that was all. It wasn't because they weren't popular; they just led completely different lifestyles than us. These guys would be running around with cigarettes hanging out their mouths, talking about drugs, sex and participating in things of questionable legality. Once after a game, Donny lit a Roman candle and chased Sean around with it, hitting him twice in the back with an active firecracker. That was crazy, dangerous stuff! On the other hand, none of us smoked, did drugs, or even got to second base with a girl. We were straight arrows. I definitely thought they were nuts (and I'm sure the rest of the guys did too), but they were a team we could play. The Fear gave us everything we needed; they were close and were always willing to compete with us.

Sean was the most normal of the bunch. Donny and Dave were loose cannons that could blow up at any moment. Think *Broad Street Bullies* and, you'll know what I'm talking about. They weren't reliable though. When they'd both show up they could carry The Fear to a win, but when neither of them came or only one showed up, we'd win easily. Ryan and Allen were crazy too, but they weren't trouble. They tried too hard to fit in with Donny and Dave, but it went against their instincts, so it just made them appear even more unusual. I remember one game at Brantwood Park, winning the opening faceoff against Allen then deaking around Sean before putting home a backhander, top cheese on Ryan. Coons must have thought it was the greatest thing he'd ever seen because he was jumping all over me yelling, "Oh my gosh! Oh my gosh!" It definitely was a sweet hands-goal, but his reaction was a little over the top, and I think it upset Ryan. Then, just a couple minutes later, Beezer simply swiped at a loose ball with one hand on the stick, and it somehow got past Ryan again. Beezer yelled, "That's the worst goal I've ever seen!" Coons was laughing it up pretty hard, and Ryan literally took his net and walked home. He didn't even take off his goalie gear or his mask or anything. He just picked up the net by the crossbar and left. It was the only time I'd ever seen someone quit like that.

I don't know if it was his learning disability or all the years of constant teasing, but Ryan was an odd duck. He'd always say the strangest things. I always tried to be nice, but having a conversation with him made me uncomfortable. Sean and Ryan played goal for them the most. I preferred when Sean was in net because if Ryan was in net, he'd start talking about porn. You would be standing in front of his net, and he'd be talking about this great movie he saw last night and how awesome the actress was. You'd just hope the play would turn around so you could run back to defence just to get away from him. Maybe he was trying to sound cool, I don't know. I just wanted to get the heck outta there. If he wasn't talking about adult movies, he was swearing. We all viewed The Fear as a team we could play, but Coons didn't care about their feelings. He'd goad Ryan and the others into overreacting all the time. Coons would tease Ryan about his voice, or his zits. Usually, Ryan would respond by giving Coons exactly what he wanted and that was an earful of, "F*** you, Coons!" Coons thought it was really funny. He would do things to bother Ryan just to get that exact response from him. Each time Ryan said those words, Coons would just laugh it off and continue to play. The following day at school, Coons would amuse himself by reciting those words in his best *Ryan voice*. He did a pretty good impression too.

Fighting was not something that happened much in the years we played. Coons had one scuff up with some jerk playing for The Fear one day, and this guy had a massive ring on his finger that damaged Coons' lip. I got in a fight with Jeff once that didn't turn out well for me. He had been giving me a hard time all game, and I'd finally had enough. I started pushing him and while I was, he wound up and clocked me right in the nose.

We wrestled a bit after that and while, on the ground we exchanged a couple blows, but he certainly landed the big one. My face was smattered with blood. It was humiliating to lose to a kid two years younger than me. Amazingly, right after the fight ended and everyone saw that Jeff and I were OK, we just went right back to playing road hockey! Other than the damage to my face there was no evidence that there had even been a fight. Beezer and I had some pretty heated battles in front of the net, but we never actually dropped our gloves. Both of us liked to go to the net, and whoever was playing defence would give it to the other. We punched and slashed the heck out of one another which was so unlike how we treated anyone else in the same position. There would always be blood on our hands whenever we'd match up in the goal mouth. Not sure why we did that. We were both competitive players, but neither of us was that ultra-competitive guy that simply would not lose. You have to be on another planet to be one of those guys. One day when the snow on the street was hard, Beezer knocked me down and from on my back I swept out his legs with a big kick and he joined me on the pavement.

Play-fighting was a different story though. Once it was too dark to play road hockey anymore, we'd start wrestling in a massive royal rumble. We knew it was time to stop playing when I'd start asking, "Where's the ball?! Where's the ball?!" It could've been right in front of me, but I still wouldn't be able to see it. Scrapping always started with someone running the goalie. Most of the time, it was Beezer jumping Venkman (even if they were on the same team). Everyone at some point would be snowed in. Somehow Beezer always managed to steal Venkman's watch like it was a game of capture the flag. I don't know how he did it with all of Venkman's goalie gear on. Maybe it was the gear that weighed Venkman down so he couldn't fight back as well.

Playing on hard, packed snow was perfect. We'd all get hyped up to play road hockey more than usual after it snowed. Southern Ontario provided the best snow conditions because it was usually heavy, wet snow that froze quickly and packed tightly. We never had to worry about it melting beneath us. Packed snow on the road enabled the goalies to slide without the resistance of the road impeding their progress. Also, it allowed the rest of us to dive to block shots and get in highlight poke checks. What we were most excited for was full body contact! No one worried about getting hit when they knew they would be landing in a snow bank. Only hard snow allowed us to do these things and it was a treat to employ them whenever we had the chance. Anything to make road hockey seem more like ice hockey was really cool.

While Coons was a solid guy who could hit hard, Venkman was the one to watch out for. He was a big fan of the hip-check and would use it all the time. I remember one time we were walking to school (not playing hockey or anything), and he just bent over and shoved his hip into my legs, sending me sprawling to the ground. He loved doing that. Once he really got me. We were having a big game on Dante, and I had the ball. I flipped one towards the net and then ran after my shot. As I was running, Venkman came out of nowhere and got me with the hip! I remember hanging upside down on his back for a few seconds before landing on the fire hydrant right in front of Pierre's house. Thankfully, it didn't hurt too much. To be honest; I kind of found it fun to get hit (without getting too banged up, of course). All of the guys thought it was incredible, especially Venkman. I remember everyone stopping and giving their take on the play. It was probably the biggest hit any of us ever doled out.

By our final year of high school (1997), playing street hockey every day became a distant memory. It was impossible to hang out every night. We no longer had that kind of time. Instead, we had to plan ahead to get the boys together for a Friday night game. We would coordinate our schedules, and all ask for the same day off so we could play. For the first time since grade four - when I hardly knew that the game existed - something other than road hockey was ruling my time. I was now governed by work and/or homework. It felt so strange to go home after school, and not get prepared for a night of road hockey. I enjoyed everything else about my last year in Brantford except the decline of street hockey. By then, only our core group of guys were playing (Beezer, Buff, Coons, Joel, The Doctor, Venkman and I). Scott, Curly and Neal didn't play anymore. The Beaver played a few times and even brought his friends a couple of times. The Beaver was in high school by now and had gotten a little bigger. Since he had played with us all his life, he was pretty confident in himself and his friends. One time he even challenged us to a game in the gym. Obviously, his team of youngsters lost to the veterans, so that was the only time he tried something like that.

CHAPTER 10

It's Only a Little Run In with the Neighbours

We played a lot of road hockey on Dante over the years, and most of the time our neighbours were good about it. Since we normally played in front of my house and Pierre's house (with Scott's on the other side), we were usually surrounded by friendly homes. However, every now and then we'd run into a problem. Every so often, we'd move the nets down in front of Venkman's house. I don't remember why we did it, but across the street from him was an elderly woman who lived alone. In the winter, we'd shovel her driveway and cut logs for her fireplace. She was a nice woman who loved to garden. She prided herself on her lawn and was really protective of it. Normally, when the ball would go onto someone's lawn, we'd send one person over to get it; they'd pick it up and put it down on the sidewalk and the game would continue. However, sometimes in the heat of the game, two guys would go after the ball and hack at it on the grass. We had been warned about this before, so the majority of the time, we honoured the polite, one person retrieval rule. The ball must have gone onto her lawn more than once that evening and the last time it did, we didn't keep the rule. Two guys went over to battle for the ball on her grass. This poor old woman came storming out of her house (in the snow, with no coat on) and started screaming at us at the top of her lungs to get off her property. She was so upset with us for doing that; I thought she was going to cry. My parents made sure I went over the next day to apologize. I had never been yelled at like that before.

Two doors down from my house were the Cumberland's. I don't remember much about them except that Mrs. Cumberland was a big lady. Typically, in road hockey, cars would drive by, and we'd pick up the nets, take them to one side of the road to let the cars pass by before resetting everything and resuming play. I hated it when the guys would drag the nets because the rough pavement would tear the twine that was wrapped around the bottom frame of the cage. It really sucked when the mesh came loose at the bottom. Balls could go right through it which would cause contention about whether or not the shot went in. Also, it meant that we would have to chase those shots down. A faulty net was not something I would tolerate for long. I would have to buy a replacement as soon as possible.

One nice, Saturday afternoon in the spring, Mrs. Cumberland was driving home and for some reason, Venkman didn't move the net. He just stared straight ahead and didn't pay any attention to her. He didn't even acknowledge that she was waiting for him to move the net. We were yelling at him to move it, but he didn't budge. Mrs. Cumberland paused for a moment longer, and then upon noticing Venkman wasn't going to do anything, she backed up a bit, then just plowed into the net with her car, sending our plastic frame flying. Being as flimsy as those nets were, I was surprised it didn't shatter. It was actually a pretty bold move on her part because Venkman didn't move as she drove through the net just behind him. Another time, Mrs. Cumberland was backing out of her driveway, and Joel fired a slapshot right off the back window of her hatchback. She stomped on the breaks, ripped open her door and reamed Joel out. Joel didn't care one bit; he just laughed the whole thing off. Even though Joel's shot wasn't strong enough to cause any damage, it was still disrespectful. I think he did it on purpose.

Nothing we ever did though could match the sheer power of Vanderwoude. Vanderwoude was another one of our friends from PJ. Vanderwoude was like Manute Bol, only without the basketball skills. This guy would have to duck to get through the doorways at school! He was probably the tallest guy I've ever stood beside. Even though he was tall, he was not an athletic guy. Maybe it was his challenging height, but sports weren't his thing. He only played street hockey with us a couple times during our senior year, but one of those times will last forever.

I remember one time I tried to set up Vanderwoude, but he missed and got really upset. He was like Coons that way, but far worse. Vanderwoude would really beat himself up over misses. However, this time his anger went to another level. For some reason, he decided a tree planted in front of a neighbour's house would be his lightning rod. He threw down his stick and then literally throttled this twelve-foot high, three-inch thick tree with both hands. Vanderwoude began to holler obscenities and violently shake the tree. While cursing, "MOTHERF***ER!" he ripped the tree in half! He then just stood there with the upper part of the trunk and the attached branches and leaves in his hands. We all stared blankly at him, as we tried to make sense of what just happened. The silence didn't last long though, within seconds we had all succumbed to unbearable laughter. This went on until we had laughed so hard that our abs and cheeks hurt. Good thing a car never came by because we weren't in a state to react to it. Vanderwoude then proceeded to calmly dump the canopy into another neighbour's backyard. The lonely upper-half stayed concealed in the backyard for a few days before it disappeared. I sure would like to know what the owner thought when he saw it hiding in the corner of his lot. I never saw the stump get removed, which was good because it would have acted as a reminder of what had happened. Ripping trees in half should be a challenge in the Strongman competitions. I'd like to see someone else try doing that!

Scott's dad was the only other neighbour we had trouble with. Whenever the ball landed on his lawn, one of us would carefully walk onto his grass, pick up the ball and bring it back to the road. As I said, we were courteous of our neighbours' properties most of the time. One time; however, Scott's dad decided he wanted to be the ultimate jerk and started raining verbal blows upon us. He began from the window in his house, then moved out onto his porch and eventually he joined us on the road. He just went on and on, calling us every name in the book. I don't think he even took a breath the whole time. Dude was obviously letting out some serious steam. We were flabbergasted because we knew we hadn't done anything wrong. After his diatribe, Venkman nonchalantly blurted out, "Blow me." In disbelief, someone challenged him, Scott's dad responded with a haughty, "What?!" I don't know why, but I jumped in and childishly replied, "He said blow him." Coons thought this was hilarious and began laughing loudly in the guy's face. Scott's dad didn't say another word. He turned on his heel, went back to his house, got on his motorcycle, and drove off. I still don't know why Coons thought what I said was so funny. It certainly was weird though. The Doctor had zero respect for Scott's dad and would shoot the ball at his parked car in the driveway all the time. Always tactful, The Doctor would make it seem like an accident even though he didn't care at all. He always made sure to respond with an arrogant, "Sorry" whenever he was asked about it.

WE ALL HAD our certain skills. Venkman was a fantastic road hockey player, but an even better goalie. His glove was the place where roof jobs went to die. Also, he loved playing the position because he enjoyed experimenting with new moves. While working the glove was his favourite, he used many different techniques as well. For Venkman, the flashier and the more daring, the better. We all saw him use big-time actions such as the pad stack, the waving glove-ly save, the desperation dive and the aggressive poke check. However, he could be a real goofball too. He could get easily distracted, and sometimes, for whatever reason, he wouldn't try as hard as he could. When he wouldn't try, it would bother me. Venkman never turned down the opportunity to play though (we even played road hockey during his mom's wedding reception!). He invited me to the reception and we were hanging out with his cousins and extended family when I noticed that we had enough kids to play a game. With many of them in their Sunday best, we got our stuff, set up the nets and started playing. We even played when we weren't on Dante. His mom used to play squash a lot at a nearby recreation club. Venkman and I would grab our mini sticks and use a Nerf ball to play in an empty squash court. He was always willing to play. Out of all the guys, he probably loved hockey the most...after me of course. I spent more time playing road hockey with Venkman than I did doing anything with anyone else.

Although mostly in goal, Venkman was also quite talented playing out because he could score. He had a hard shot and a quick release. Only once did it get him in trouble. One night I was over at his house watching Montreal and Hartford play game seven of the Adams division semi-finals on TV. We watched Gilbert Dionne score a beautiful goal on Frank Pietrangelo. During intermission, we tried to recreate it ourselves in his driveway. On his first attempt, Venkman spun and rifled the ball right through his garage door! That perfectly round hole at the bottom of the door testified of Venkman's powerful shot. We both looked at the hole, then at each other. Without saying a word, we quietly put the equipment away and went back inside to watch the second period. His mom must not have heard the shot because she didn't say anything. The next day, I asked Venkman if he wanted to play ball hockey after school, but he said he couldn't because his mom was making him spackle up the hole. He did a good job too. Even years later you could only see the repaired spot if you knew what you were looking for.

Joel didn't possess the physical abilities that Venkman did, but he always worked hard. You could easily motivate Joel, and he'd do whatever he could to get better. I remember one time I created a ranking chart for all the guys. I was inspired by *Super Nintendo's* NHL video games where they would give pros a certain grade for skating, shooting, speed, aggression and overall skill. I developed rankings for all the guys road hockey skills based on the same criteria. It was a stupid thing to do because it made some guys feel pretty bad about themselves. Joel was already, without question, the slowest guy among us. He played ice hockey for years, road hockey with us, and was a darn good baseball player too. However, he was not blessed with speed. We'd pick on him about his lack of speed all the time. It wasn't just his foot-speed either; his wind-up was slower than the day was long. Joel was a smart dude though, very precise and analytical. Because of that, even when he spoke, it could take a while for him to express himself. After I ranked him low on speed and aggression, Joel decided to act more aggressively during games. He knew he couldn't improve his speed, but his aggression was something he could work on. Joel was bigger than most of us, so he started to use his frame to his advantage. He began leaning on us to gain possession and to win ball battles.

Joel was very strong at face-offs, but he wasn't limited to just that. He could score goals too. His shot was all right, but he missed a lot. Typically, Joel would defend his wayward attempt by suggesting he "just" missed. Well, he "just" missed all the time then. I'm not sure if he missed the net as much as Coons, but he definitely missed a great deal! One evening on White Owl, Joel's shot was so far off target, it shattered Buff Dude's porch light. The net wasn't even facing the light fixture! Another time, playing in my driveway, Joel missed so much that there were literally twenty-eight dents in my garage door. Despite what these damages may say, he didn't have a powerful shot, but Joel could still score. He scored in each of our three on three tournaments and was probably the Black Bears all-time, tournament-scoring leader. To top that off, he was a sensational, money goalie during those times too.

His Royal Buffness was a versatile guy. Buff Dude grew up playing soccer, and it showed. He had iron lungs and was fast. He also could play a few different instruments thanks to all the practice he got from performing in his church band. Even though Buff Dude was a year younger than the rest of us, you'd never know it. He was always there and never looked out of place in anything we did, whether it was playing street hockey or just hanging out. No question, Buff was the smallest and lightest among us, although he did grow taller than Beezer by the end of high school. Regardless of his stature, whenever someone hit him, he never got hurt. He could bounce back faster than we could recover from delivering the hit. Buff was smart and earned some good grades in school, but this one time, the poor guy really got burned. He went into his grade twelve, final math exam with a mark over 80%. I can remember talking to him the day of the final, and he seemed ready to go. What happened next was one of the worst crashes I'd ever seen. Even though he participated in the exam, Buff's final mark landed in the sixties. Somehow, Buff totally biffed it on his exam. I'm not one to talk though. I went into my grade ten English exam with an eighty-five and with no viable explanation, missed the exam and received a zero. I still passed, but it sucked going from an "A" to a "C."

It's funny how things work out. Buff Dude grew up a staunch Leaf fan, but when he moved to Calgary (after high school) and watched the Flames go to the finals in '04, he became a Flamers fan. Of course, I grew up cheering for Calgary, but transformed into a huge Leafs fan while attending university. Toronto was a lot of fun to watch in the late '90s. Once Gilmore joined the Buds in '92, Leaf Nation really expanded. Just about everyone in high school was wearing Blue and White and Buff fit right in. It wasn't that bad cheering for Calgary during that time because they had a good team too. That was until the playoffs. Toronto was winning a couple of rounds and Calgary was winning a couple of games.

I've never met anyone as brash as Coons when he was young. His personality was so different from the rest of my friends, but we shared so many similarities that we became good friends right away. I used to attend seminary every morning before school, and once class was over, I'd go over to Coons' house. We'd hang out there for a bit before catching the bus to high school. We'd sit in his living room and listen to golden oldies on the radio. He really got to know his oldies this way. When *Die Hard with a Vengeance* came out, it opened with a song titled: *Summer in the City*. One day I asked him who performed this catchy tune. (Remember, this is 1995, no Internet and the song was close to thirty-years-old.) Without hesitation, Coons responded with, *"The Lovin' Spoonful"*, as if I should've known that.

Coons was a very confident guy. He didn't care what he said or how he looked. He was very interested in girls from the moment I met him, but he never acted on it. Girls would throw themselves at Coons, but it never fazed him. The rest of us would've killed to get that kind of feminine attention. Heck, I was excited when his female admirers would talk to me, just because I was his friend. Many of these girls were pretty hot too, and they gave him so much admiration it was like he was paying them to ogle him. Although I wouldn't call him a bad boy, I think the chicks thought he was one, and they liked that.

Another thing that separated Coons from the rest of us was his gas. You've heard the term, "Clear a room?" Coons actually did; I was there. After finishing his fish and chip lunches, Coons would come back to the geography hall at PJ, and hang out with us. We never ate in the cafeteria. We'd all just get our lunches and eat together in the hall. The geography hall wasn't a long hallway, and it had double doors at both ends. Coons would sit on the floor with his knees bent, and whether it was on purpose or not, he would let 'em rip. Every day this happened. No one appreciated it, but we all laughed every time. Coons would just sit there and fart. He loved seeing our reactions; watching our reactions was like entertainment for him.

One time, one of his farts was so powerful that the ten of us in the hall thought we were suffocating! Moments later – as we were gasping between breaths and laughter – a group of girls walked into the hall. Almost as quickly as they opened the door, the four of them caught a whiff of the stench and turned around. It was hilarious! However, the best Coons' fart was in a grocery store. Sometimes, Joel, Coons and I would walk to the grocery store right across the street from the school. We walked into the main entrance where people were picking up their shopping carts when Coons declared, "Unleash the beast!" His fart was so loud it stopped traffic. Joel was appalled and embarrassed by the action. On the other hand, I thought it was hilarious. I lost my mind; I could not stop laughing. Joel muttered something derogatory and then left in disgust. Coons never blinked an eyelash. When he wasn't farting, Coons was a good road hockey player. He had the hardest shot and was our fastest runner (except for those two years when Fumie was around). Coons loved playing with us. I don't think he ever missed a game during those five years of high school. If it hadn't been for his temper, Coons might have been the perfect player.

Beezer was the one who started it all. I can remember going over to his house in the fifth grade and picking which hockey cards we liked best based on their pictures. If the picture on the card wasn't exciting, we figured it wasn't worth anything, so we discarded it. I can clearly remember burning Brendan Shanahan's rookie card because it was just a mug shot and not an action photo. Given that Brett Hull's rookie card is found in the same set of that year, and his photo is just as uninspiring; I probably burned that one too. Beezer got me into hockey; I got Venkman into hockey, and hockey strengthened the existing friendship I had with Joel. Joel used road hockey to add Coons and Fumie to our group and Beezer brought Buff Dude into the gang because of hockey too.

For years, Beezer was easily our best player. Small but strong, Beezer could do it all. He wasn't good in net, but he'd go in every once and while just for a laugh. He was very athletic and smart as a whip. Beezer was a good teammate. His shot was OK, but he used his speed and his head to create plays. He would rack points up himself and make others around him better. Sometimes Beezer was overly sarcastic, but he never said anything really mean to anyone. It was too bad for us that he took a road hockey sabbatical for a year, but I guess he needed it at the time. I suppose Beezer was a little more typical than the rest of us. Never once did I consider myself or my friends too old for road hockey. Even though Beezer gave up for a while (to be with girls and dumb things like smoking), the bottom line was he came back, and we were all happy he did.

ROAD HOCKEY WASN'T the only way to play. We all loved hockey so much that we played a game called Hand Hockey in my basement. My dad told us it was a game he used to play as a kid. Once Neal and I started to show an interest in hockey my dad decided to demonstrate this new game to us. Hand Hockey was played on your hands and knees, using your hand to swat a Nerf ball past your opponent. Sometimes we would actually bring the road hockey nets into my basement, but it was rare. Most of the time, we used the back of the couch and the wall parallel to it as our nets. The size of the goal was the full width of the couch, so about seven-feet long, but only the bottom two feet of the couch counted towards scoring. I loved to play Hand Hockey. I would go through pants like crazy because all the friction from the carpet would burn holes in the knees. Neal and I played a lot when we were younger, but as we got older, it took too much persuading and so I didn't ask him as much. This was too bad because Neal was good. Venkman was good too – too good. It was like five goals, ten saves, I couldn't beat Venkman at Hand Hockey. Sometimes I'd have all the guys over, and we'd have tournaments. This was always fun because the game was so simple yet entertaining. We'd always have a good time when we played Hand Hockey. In Hand Hockey, there were no teammates, and you were limited to maybe ten feet between the two of you, so you'd either had to shoot with your strong hand, "pass it" with your weak hand and try your luck with a one-timer, or "go to the backhand." We tried things like slicing the ball similar to the way you would in tennis. You might be able to fool the other guy with the shot, but when it hit the ground the ball would stop, and very rarely have the gas to cross the line (or hit the couch). We also experimented with, "the pillow pads." We would take two regular bed pillows and attach them to each of our legs using neckties or belts. Pillow pads were Buff's idea. They were great because they saved our knees. (I swear I didn't have hair on my lower legs until I was twenty-two.) However, like our street hockey pads, the pillow pads could spin around on our leg which was very uncomfortable. In the end, Hand Hockey long outlasted the use of pillow pads.

Every so often, we'd get a big game together and play full-basement Hand Hockey. We'd push the couch all the way to the other end of the room, right up against the fireplace. This would make the playing surface thirty-feet which was large enough to hold teams of two on two or even three on three. With games this large, we'd do all sorts of things to change it up like using the walls to angle passes or shots. We also tried using a racquetball. Racquetballs drastically increased the speed of the game. Man, those little things could really fly! Shooting a racquetball off the wall was almost as crazy as using a super ball. Nerf balls weighed nothing, so no one got hurt whenever we used them. However, racquetballs caused a lot of damages. There were times when guys got sacked or got hit in the eye by them. On a couple of occasions, the racquetball was fired into a picture on the wall, shattering the glass all over the floor. My parents never got too upset even though this happened more than once. I'm not sure what teens do today, but I assume not many of them would spend time playing games like we did. We loved playing Hand Hockey. It was one of our favourite things to do when it was too dark outside to play road hockey.

CHAPTER 11

I've Still Got a Lot of Road Hockey Left In Me

Road hockey didn't end at high school. Other than Venkman, the guys all stuck close to home while attending post-secondary. Joel was in Toronto but came home often. Coons was in Hamilton, and he was always home. Beezer and Buff Dude worked for a year before going to school. I worked full-time for six months before beginning my missionary service. We would play a couple of times a month, usually in a rented gym. By this time in our lives, competition was minimal and had been entirely replaced with camaraderie. The battles in front of the net were more about trying to get the other guy to laugh and lose control, rather than trying to knock him on his trash. Besides, road hockey was all we ever did growing up, and it would've been weird if someone suggested anything else.

I can remember playing five goals, ten saves with Beezer as my last act of road hockey before surrendering my hockey obsession for two years while I served a full-time mission. Beezer was a good athlete, but that did not translate over when he put the pads on. Sometimes, when you don't try, and expectations are low it can have unprecedented results. I think they call this getting lucky. Well, Beezer was dang lucky! I was labelling shots, and he was pulling them out of mid-air like he was picking cherries. I went easy on him to start, but it cost me because it came down to the last shot. I ripped one destined for the top corner, but Beezer flung his glove out like he was swatting at a fly, and he just managed to deflect the ball away from the goal... and win. I was stunned. This defeat coming just months after my most triumphant victory over Venkman in the same game. Losing to Venkman a million times was better than losing to Beezer once. Venkman was a goalie, and he knew how to get in my head. Beezer was not a goalie, and he never claimed to be, but he got away with that one. Worst of all, I knew he would never let me get away with it. It was always good-natured ribbing, but still, he clung to this victory like a winning lottery ticket.

I spent the first eleven months of 1998 serving a mission before I badly injured my knee and needed to return home for surgery. It took four months to get the operation, and then another three months of physio before I could fully use the joint again, so I never went back to the mission. While recovering, no one could resist the desire to play again. On Christmas break, 1998 (a month before my surgery), we gathered up everyone and strung a few games together on White Owl. Our itch to play road hockey was simply something that we could not overcome. Just like a physical itch, you can delay the need to scratch for a few seconds, maybe longer, if you're strong enough, but eventually the urge persists and action is required. With a torn ACL, I couldn't do much more than stand in front of the net and whack rebounds away every once in a while. Although I was forced to watch most of the game from a seat in the snow, it was a good game. Only about a year had passed since we had all played together, but it felt like much longer. Perhaps it felt this way because, for the first time in our lives, we had all gone more than a month without playing road hockey. It was an addiction that was cut off cold turkey, but then tasted so delicious to return to again.

After knee surgery, I recovered quickly and was able to go to school in the fall of 1999. I attended the University of Ottawa and lived with a nice family in their basement suite. The man who owned the house was also my bishop. He introduced me to Wednesday night floor hockey at the church. University floor hockey was great. I had no idea that I'd find so many other guys that enjoyed street hockey like I did. Each week we had at least ten guys willing to play. We had serious goalies with full gear, full-sized nets instead of road hockey nets and best of all, everyone shared a remarkable balance between competition and sportsmanship.

Playing against strangers after so many years of only playing with the same group of guys was unusual and even intimidating at times, but I soon found out that I really had nothing to fear. I was like King Clancy to these guys. I could play the role of the unbeatable 'tender or deadly sharpshooter. During high school road hockey with the guys, I showed the ability to dance through a whole team and finish off, but it was rare. In Ottawa though, I did it every week! It became a regular practice for me to bury one fabulous goal a game. Running around guys required speed, but waltzing through them took quickness and creativity. The regulars came to expect it after a couple months of routine dangling. I'd start a rush and the other goalie would yell at his teammates to, "Watch out for him!" It was church floor hockey, so there was no body contact. We could stand guys up, but there was no hitting. This made dangling a little easier. If a player stepped in front of me to block my way, I could undress him without worrying about getting knocked off the ball. When contact is involved, I would have elected to shoot right past the defender, but it's so much more fun to carry the ball right through guys.

I'm not sure how, but I became a faster runner in university than I was during high school. I don't know if my body was maturing or what, but I started to outrun guys I never thought I could a few years before. I used this newly discovered gear to help me burn guys on the rush. Of course, I continued to track my stats using twenty-five game blocks, just as I used to. It never felt weird that I was the only one doing it.

One goal really sticks out in my mind, and it was the result of swift hands. I was a right-hand shot standing on the left wing goal line, about three-feet off the near post.

The ball bounced off the wall behind the net and came right to me. Without hesitation, I whipped it right under the bar and in. It was an acute angle and the goalie was over in time to cover, but not upstairs over the shoulder. I received a well-deserved congrats from everyone there (even the victimized goalie).

Floor hockey at a church had rules. Being kind and keeping the language G-rated went without saying, however; there was another law that took some adjustment for most of us. It was vital that the stick blade not come in direct contact with the floor. Most church gyms are used for basketball and volleyball and thus, have a very nice, wood floor that would get banged up from hockey sticks if there was no protection. Church leaders allowed us to play if we used something on our blades to prevent damage to the floor. In all my years of playing road hockey, the only thing about my blades that I worried about was how often I had to replace them. The asphalt was unforgiving on wooden blades, and it ground them down in no time. I've seen way too many guys trying to use an old wooden blade in road hockey and getting frustrated with them from all the fanning that followed.

To protect the church floor from my stick, I first tried a couple of layers of good old duct tape. The "Handy Man's Secret Weapon" had worked well for us on goalie equipment, but it failed to hold up here. The tape wore off faster than it took me to apply it. I needed a better plan. Next, I tried wrapping a dish cloth around the blade. The rag fell apart in no time. I managed to get my hands on an old, thick blanket and cut out a chunk. This blanket was so chunky, I thought it would last forever. I was sure this was my solution. The blanket did last longer than the tape and the rag, but it didn't make it past a few games. It was so bulky that I felt it was hindering my shot, so once it fell off, I didn't put it on again. Then one of the guys told me to use denim. For the sake of the game, I sacrificed my jeans. I remember trying to cut as inconspicuously as I could, but there was no denying it, my pants were not long enough anymore. At least the denim worked. I wrapped just enough to cover the underside of the blade and taped it on. That strip of denim lasted the rest of the year.

My roommate was a dude named Tony. He was a lanky fellow that enjoyed hockey too. A couple of times a week he'd come home from work late, wake me up at 01:00 and ask if I wanted to play floor hockey. Even at this hour, I'd readily accept. Tony worked at a restaurant and would be just finishing his shift when he felt the hockey craving. He'd already have a few guys lined up to play before asking me, and the rest was easy. We would borrow the bishop's keys to the church (that he always left hanging in the hallway), and we'd be off. Our small gang would make the short walk over to the church and let ourselves in. We'd bring a radio and blast *Eye of the Tiger* while we played. The most people we ever got out to these ghastly hour games was five, but I remember having a lot of fun during these games. We'd pack up after an hour or two; then I'd bag a few Z's before heading to class the next morning.

Tuesdays were always brutal. I lived forty minutes away from the university and although it gave me a lot of time to read on the bus; it meant longer days. Tuesday's classes started at 08:00, and I'd have almost continuous classes until 16:00. Then, I had a long three-hour break before my only night class of the year. I'd finish class at 21:00 and catch one of the late buses heading back to my home in Orleans. Ottawa has the most fantastic transit system I've ever used. In those days, you could find a bus going your way every five minutes, twenty-one hours a day. I'd go home to grab a bite before going back to university for my radio show which ran from midnight to 04:00. My show was called, "Time Warp" because I played obscure stuff from the '60s and '70s. Most of the time, I never heard of the band I was playing, but it was the only time I could get on the air, so listening to bad music was the penalty. I'm not bilingual, and Ottawa is definitely more French- than English-speaking, so this made finding a job where bilingualism wasn't required very tough. At least I spoke the universal Canadian language of hockey fluently. I would spend just about every break between songs talking about it; scores, news, opinions, everything, even though I don't think anyone ever listened to my show. My friends would say they'd listen, but they always admitted they fell asleep. Even I did once. It was close to the end of my show as I put on a new track. I looked out the window and saw nothing but darkness. That sight alone added forty pounds to my eyelids, so I put my feet up on the console, leaned back in my chair and dozed off. At the time, I rationalized my decision by thinking the music would keep me semi-awake. However, I remember waking up to dead air and scrambling to break the silence in the most professional, sleepy voice I had. I don't know how long I was out for, my best guess is five minutes, but I'll never know for sure. Fortunately, no one was listening, and no one found out.

After my show, I'd wait until the first bus arrived at 04:40, and take it home. I'd then finish my homework until 07:00. The next hour would be spent getting ready for the new day, followed by a bus ride to school for class at 10:00. Classes were easy on Wednesday; I'd be home by 14:00. I would then do more homework until 20:00 when it was time for floor hockey at the church. It didn't matter if things were due, and/or I was falling asleep standing up, I was always ready to play, and I always did. By the time I'd get to bed on Wednesday nights, I would have been up for nearly forty hours straight. It was so worth it. I loved hockey, so I was glad to do it!

Tony and I took the floor hockey at the gym another obsessive step further. Since we had a group of dedicated guys playing each week, we decided to create a tournament. Tony and I entered our midnight mob as one team, and the rest of the regulars banded together on a few other teams until we had four in total. The night before the tournament, Tony and I created a replica of the Stanley Cup using things around the house. We used an old five gallon paint bucket as the base and a couple one litre yogurt cups as the neck. We wrapped them in tin foil and glued a silver salad bowl on top. To be honest, it looked pretty darn good, and it got everyone excited to play for it.

We played a lot of floor hockey that day. Our tournament was a typical round robin style, where everyone played each other once, followed by a one versus four and two versus three semi-final and eventually one final, championship game. We did not have a very balanced team. Tony wasn't that good, while the other two guys on the team were specialists. One guy was a great goal-scorer, but he just cherry picked. The other was only a defensive player and didn't leave the front of the net. Therefore, I was forced to play both ways at all times, which was exhausting. Some may say that playing road hockey several times a week for all five years of high school is dedicated. Others might say playing at 01:00 is committed. But I'd say this tournament was when I was driven to play hockey more than ever. Maybe it was the cup, maybe it was playing so hard both ways and really allowing the team to lean on me heavily, but I just remember working harder and caring more than ever before. I had my first of four knee surgeries the year before coming to Ottawa, and although I was feeling good, this tournament brought out the worst in that joint. I can remember diving to break up plays and blocking shots while attacking both ends to the point where my legs were numb. I could still use my legs, but I couldn't feel them much. I'd have so much difficulty that I would need to use the net to help me get up. I'd have to literally use all of my strength and all my will to get into the play. My wife thinks I'm a masochist for doing stuff like this, but it was all worth it at the time. My team was eliminated in the semis, losing 5-2. I had one goal in that game- a one-timer (thanks, Coons) - but it was more fun to see the winning team have a good time with the cup I helped to create. The champs even took our fake Stanley out with them in the back of a pickup truck and drove around flashing it to the neighbourhood.

From my experience, I'd say Ottawa is the best place in the world for shinny hockey. The city produced small rinks all over the place; there were two close to my house, which I'd use all the time. City crews kept the ice fresh and clean. They even built boards around it and put up the nets. In a few places, the shinny rinks were even better because they were larger, had heated change rooms and big outdoor lights. There would be so many people out there you could hardly move, but it was so much fun. To this day, even after living in all three of the Prairie Provinces for a long time now, I've never seen a city so committed to providing shinny rinks to the community like Ottawa does.

My time in Ottawa wasn't too long. I transferred to Lethbridge, Alberta the next year to continue my education. At school, I continued my floor hockey participation. The problem with school-sponsored events was the degree of safety involved. It was back to those floppy, plastic sticks and no slapshots. Still, it was hockey, it was once a week, and it was fun.

My journalism classmates were my teammates, and we called ourselves the "Spread Eagles" (only a college team would think of and get away with something like that!). We had some athletic guys playing for us, and I thought we'd do OK. The only problem was that we were short a goalie. Although it wasn't my favourite spot to play, since no one on my team wanted to play goal, I was forced to strap 'em on to save the game. I don't know how, but I was pretty good. (Looking back on these things now. I suppose the guys I grew up with were just better than a lot of others because I was terrible when I played goal in high school, but since then, many have considered me a good goalie.) I played in net the first few games, and we won them all. As our confidence grew, one of the other guys decided he'd like to strap on the pads. This was perfect! I saw how good I was in net against the other teams and thought, "If I can outplay these teams while in a position I'm not good at, I can dominate if I play forward."

The thought turned to action, and I went out for the rest of the season semester. Although I'd hardly call it a gamble (because it was a sound decision) when I played forward, I bagged goals almost at will. It was great! I was firing shots in from anywhere, and since it was a co-ed league, I was garnering the attention of the ladies in attendance (it was the closest I ever got to having puck-bunnies). I actually had guys from the other team ask me how I got to be so good! I felt like an all-star, and it was pretty great. My team was unbeatable during the regular season, and I ran away with the league scoring crown.

Sadly, the experiment didn't last long and in a rather humbling experience, I damaged my knees playing intramural floor hockey. While chasing down a loose ball, some dude stuck his stick out, and I stepped on his plastic blade. My knees buckled, and I crashed awkwardly into the cement wall. I tore the medial meniscus in both knees, and they both were operated on soon after. This would make it three knee surgeries in two years. To compare myself to Bobby Orr – the greatest hockey player to ever live– would be egotistical, pompous and just entirely incorrect. So, let's say I'm like Gord Kluzak. Gordie was a first overall pick of the Bruins in 1982, but more knee surgeries than years played ended his great hockey hopes far too soon. To be realistic and fair to Gordie though, Kluzak was aiming for a Stanley Cup, and I was just wanted to play floor hockey for as long as possible.

When I'd come back to Ontario during the summers, the guys and I, would plan a game or two. My parents' garage had moved from Brantford to Burlington, but still held all the goalie gear - although the stuff would be considered archaic by then – so the guys would travel in for a game. We'd rent out a gym and go for it. We all made new friends going to different universities and a few times we'd have new faces participating in our games. The passion for road hockey still existed between us then, even though we played significantly less than we used to and even less with one another.

One summer day in 2001, we tried to rent a gym, but they were just about to close. After walking outside the building, some guy ran up to me and said he worked at the facility and heard we wanted the gym. He told me that if we all showed up twenty minutes after the building closed, he'd let us in the back door. He also told us the parking lot was filmed by CC video, and we'd have to make it look like we were leaving, or the cameras could tip off management. Feeling like a bunch of undercover athletes, the ten of us huddled up and walked across the big parking lot and disappeared behind trees and hedges on the other side. After twenty minutes, we took a long, alternate way back to the gym where the guy let us in. We paid this dude a hundred dollars for two hours which was better than the regular fee and pure, under the table profit for him, so we were all really happy with the arrangement.

After finishing my post-secondary education, floor hockey only occurred just a couple of times a year. Once though, Venkman, Coons, Beezer and I used the gym at the church in Burlington to play. We couldn't really have a game with only four guys, but we did the best we could, and had fun with it. Beezer went in goal. I finally had my opportunity to avenge my loss to Beezer! The pain of loss from our initial encounter five years previous was still throbbing. I played a lot of floor hockey in university, but Beezer did too. I'd say out of all of us; we certainly played the most. Still, Beezer wasn't a good goalie, and there was no way I was going to go easy on him. I got out to a big lead with three goals in my first six shots and was feeling good. It was 4-7 for me, and then somehow, Dominick Hasek's spirit took over

Beezer's body. He made three saves in a row. To this day, I still can't figure out how he did it. I can remember each save so clearly, the memory remains like it was a life-changing, terrifying nightmare.

The first attempt, I raced in and did my Joe Nieuwendyk impression. Nieuwendyk had this move where he'd go in showing backhand all the way, only to pull it back to his forehand at the last second and sweep it in. It was hard to do in running shoes, but I still got a good shot away. Unfortunately, Beezer lunged out with his big left pad and kicked it away. The save had left him down and vulnerable, so I rapidly chased down the rebound, spun and fired a low shot targeted just inside the near post. It was a great shot, but somehow, Beezer dove back, crammed the pipe and just barely kept it from completely crossing the line. Everything came down to this last shot. If it was a goal, I'd get my well-deserved and overdue payback, but if it was a save, then Beezer would move to 2-0 lifetime against me.

I came in fast and gave him the forehand look. Beezer took the bait and committed to his left. I then proceeded to move to the backhand and I can't believe how much of the net I'm looking at! There's so much and the joy of winning was so close I'm already celebrating in my head; all I have to do was slide her home. All this seems to happening now in slow motion. Once real time picked up, I saw Beezer's glove nudge the rolling ball out of the way using his glove hand. I couldn't believe it! Coons shouted, "Oh the Hasek save!" Beezer had flipped and contorted his body like the Dominator would to pull off an inhuman save. If I had raised the shot even six inches, it would have gone in, but instead, the ball hit a small portion of the leather and was diverted away from the net. I'm not kidding when I say I was grief stricken. I seriously had reoccurring nightmares of that moment that roused me from my sleep for several months. Losing to Venkman hundreds of times became so common that it was a laughable losing streak, but I wasn't laughing here. Oh, but I'm sure Beezer is having a good laugh over this right now as he recalls each historic stop in his own memory hall of fame. I give him full marks though because he really did make some miraculous saves. I believe he duly earned this second win, much more than the first.

CHAPTER 12
Getting Paid to Play

My first job out of school was in radio as a hockey play-by-play announcer for *CKDM* in Dauphin, Manitoba for the *Manitoba Junior Hockey League (MJHL)*. It was my dream career. I had wanted to call hockey games since I was thirteen! I was so happy to see that dream bear fruit. It was a great job because I was surrounded by hockey. I was around the game and the players all day. I remember the smell of the rink becoming this rejuvenating elixir. All the business of the day was over, and now I was in my wheel-house. It was wonderful to walk into one of those old barns and know that for the next five hours I'd only have to watch and talk about hockey. It really was a dream come true.

Those five years I spent covering junior hockey really elevated my understanding of the game. Some coaches were really great to talk to. They'd point out stuff about positioning, posture and design I never considered before. I remember talking to one coach who had a small, but very talented player on his team. I asked him what he planned to do to get this player away from traffic and harassment of the opposing team. The coach made a cross-checking gesture and said, "Make the other guy a beaver." I was surprised by this. "Won't he get a penalty though?" I said. The coach responded, "Maybe, but that other guy won't go after him again." I was only thinking about the short-term while the coach was obviously looking well beyond that one play.

It was great going on the road and getting to know the players. Even as teenagers, some of them were very mature. Most of them would not go on to play pro, and they knew that, so they treasured their time. Some were very active in the community and put on programs for kids. Other times though, they acted their age and maybe even younger. Hockey players love pranks, and they got me once.

It was the opening round of the 2002 playoffs between Dauphin and the *OCN Blizzard*. OCN played out of The Pas, and they had a great team. The Blizzard easily won the division. They had the league's top point-getter and goal-scorer to go along with the overall best record, but they were really known for their fans. OCN had a rink unlike most other rinks because the seats had plywood in front of the first row that went all around the building. It was probably there for safety, but the rowdy fans would pound on the wood, and it was loud. It sounded more like a gladiator arena than a hockey rink. I couldn't even hear my programmer back at the station telling me the commercial was over and that I was live due to the immense noise. People told me the next day that there would be periods of the broadcast when all they could hear was the crowd, or I'd be mid-sentence when the break was over because I guessed to early when the commercial was over and I'd just start calling the game again.

In the morning before game one of the series, I met the team at the visiting arena to interview them. The coach told me just to wait a bit before interviewing anyone because he wanted to talk to the troops first. He asked me to wait at ice-level and told me they'd be out soon. So, I left the hallways and went inside the rink. I just sat there in the dark, empty rink for a while and waited. I waited a long time but figured the coach must have been really firing the guys up, so I didn't want to disturb them. I continued to wait. I wasn't bored though. Just as much as the players wanted to be sharp, I wanted to be as well. I knew it would be a crazy house in a few hours and I wanted to put on a good broadcast. So, I continued to wait. After an hour, I thought that the guys must have been getting geared up for a game day skate and that I'd see them walking through the door at any moment. After another hour passed, I finally decided I'd go and see what was taking them so long. I left the rink and went to the visitor's dressing room only to find it empty. Where the heck was everyone?! I searched the arena, but no one was there. I sheepishly left the building and went back to the hotel trying to figure out how I messed up. Once I reached the hotel, I found out what happened. The team was waiting for me in the lobby and yelled, "Gotcha!" Secretly, the coach had escorted the whole team out only to make me wait. They all couldn't believe how long I had waited. It was their most well-executed play of the series.

I really enjoyed doing play-by-play, but I also enjoyed creating game notes. This would be the research I would do before games. I would prepare my own stats about both teams so I would have things to talk about other than the play itself. Back in the early 2000s, the *MJHL* didn't keep up on stats like they do now. The newsroom would receive a fax once a week about scoring leaders and other such details. It wasn't enough for me, so I would take hours each day updating my own scoring leaders, goaltending leaders, special team percentages and much more. To do it, I would have to dive into the boxscores of each game and dig out the details for every single player. Although it sounds tedious, I loved it. I was the only reporter in the league that could provide such an advanced level of knowledge of player and team stats across the whole league and for every game. I had up-to-date details but also trends, streaks and information about all players, not just the leaders. Other journalists tried to catch up. By the next season, the league began to do it themselves. It was special for me to think I started a movement that improved the media relations and elevated the commitment of all the journalists in the league.

I became a bit of a local and regional celebrity as a hockey play-by-play announcer. I didn't care for it, or need the attention, but it was always very flattering when someone would tell me they enjoy listening to my broadcasts. My celebrity was nice when the radio station would get involved in community activities, whether charitable or just promotional. We had a slow-pitch team in the city league, a curling team and on one special occasion, a road hockey team.

It was 2004 and the local *Myers Norris Penny* (MNP), was the lead sponsor in a co-ed, three on three, road hockey charity event. I put a team together that included two of my co-workers and one friend, but we still entered under the name of the radio station. There were six teams in this event and the winner was awarded a trophy. After a round robin, there were two semi-finals, followed by the championship game. Each game, was fifteen minutes long, and the leader, after the time ran out won the game. MNP had won the tournament three of the first four years and some of those past champions were still playing for their team. There were no public teams, only businesses, entered and so each team was named after a business.

Our little team was anchored by our morning show host, Noeller. This dude was the most competitive guy I'd ever met. He was so intense during any sport; he could get really upset sometimes. Even during Slo-Pitch, he would throw his hat, or bat if he or someone else made a mistake. He was a great guy though. Noeller was a very generous and thoughtful guy. Some of those qualities just sort of separated themselves from him during a game. Noeller loved sports, and he knew how to play. He used his show to promote the event and our team. The second member of the crew was Katherine. All the floor hockey I played in Lethbridge was co-ed, so I knew that for most of the time, the girls playing would prefer to just play D. Katherine was a volleyball player in high school and was probably the best female athlete available to us, so Noeller and I were very happy to have her. Our last member was a bit of a ringer. Adam grew up in playing ice hockey and even played goal at the Midget 'AAA' level, holding the local team record for most shots faced in a season. He hadn't played hockey in a few years, but he was still in good shape. To be fair, we decided not to use him in net though.

Our first game was too easy. Despite not playing regular road hockey for a couple years by now, I had no problem picking the game up again. Although not as elaborate as some of the other tournaments I'd been in, MNP did a good job. They divided their parking lot into two playing surfaces. The boards were bales of straw, which really made me laugh. I had grown up in southern Ontario, and the straw bales just screamed small town hickville. Oh well, I didn't care. I was there with my team, and getting to play road hockey was going to be better than anything else I could be working on that day. With Noeller in net, we dominated our first opponents representing *Home Hardware*. We averaged close to a goal a minute, and I scored half of them.

Our second game should've been the easiest one, but it turned out to be a real nail-biter. We took on the *Friendship Centre* whose goalie was armed with kitchenware instead of street hockey equipment. She had frying pans latched to her arms and legs and pot lids stuck to her stick to add a little more coverage. It was unlike anything I had ever seen on the street. We knew they lost their first game and after crushing our first opponent, we figured we'd roll over these guys too. Pride is the worst feature a team or individual can have when facing competition. It turned out we played far too nicely and found ourselves tied in a low-scoring affair. I had several chances to score all game, but was continually turned aside by the cafeteria keeper. Noeller was freaking out! He couldn't believe I could light it up so well in one game then go stone cold in the very next match. To be honest, I was freaking out too, but I wasn't manifesting it the same way Noeller was. Thankfully, we had a secret weapon (that was not Adam). Katherine scored late to bump us to a 4-3 win to remain undefeated. I swear I almost kissed her after that goal! There was literally a sigh of relief among our group after almost blowing what should've been a walk in the park.

Obviously, this tournament was very different than the paid ones I competed in during high school. Paid tournament teams were filled with junior players that made us look like atom level competitors. We had to really try hard in those tournaments. We ensured we practiced and gave our goalies the best equipment we could muster. In this MNP tournament, teams were pretty relaxed; no physical stuff whatsoever. No one showboated or talked trash. It was about as friendly as you could get between two teams that both wanted to win.

As the local radio station, we faced a lot of pressure. Everyone knew who we were and knew no matter what happened, the stories from this event would be going to air. As Sports Director, everyone knew me and assumed that since I was a sport's guy that I must be good at sports. Although not all sport's guys are good at sports, that was the perception. We knew some of our opponents, but for the most part they were just regular guys with regular jobs. They all wanted to be the team to knock off the big radio station. That would be the icing on their cake. We could see it in their eyes. We watched other teams play when we were between games, and teams definitely cranked up their mojos when they lined up against team CKDM.

Our third game didn't start well. For one, we took Noeller out of the net because I wanted to go in. During university, I became a decent goalie and although it had been a couple years, I thought I still was. However, I had somehow reverted back to my high school goaltending skills amid this layoff. This is how bad I had become. During warm ups, I didn't stop a single shot! And I was trying! After allowing a dozen or so shots get by me, I pulled the plug. My teammates agreed that the experiment wasn't working. It was so bad that we had to put Noeller back in at the last second. The third game against *Co-Op* wasn't as challenging as the previous, but not a blow out like our first game. We had learned not to be prideful. We attempted to stay consistent. I got a little of my scoring touch back and had another hat trick, but Adam was our biggest offensive supplier. He scored five in an 8-5 win.

The semis were fun. We took on *BMO*. One of their guys was an active volunteer and on the board for the local junior team I covered. He was a great guy who was always in my corner whenever small issues arose between the radio station and the team. As we expected, this was a close one. BMO put up a good fight and actually controlled the game to start, but I think our youthful bodies caught up with them. Our average age was early twenties - by far the youngest in this tournament - whereas BMO's average age was twice ours. Nevertheless, they jumped out to a 4-2 lead but once they got gassed, we were able to pour it on. I lit them up for five goals myself and we won 10-6.

The finals pitted us against MNP. They were good. Although we both were unbeaten in the round robin, they finished first because they had a wider goal differential than us. To be honest, I wasn't that confident going in. We knew we only won the semi-final game because the older guys ran out of juice. It was unlikely that we would get that lucky again, especially against the hosts and defending champs. We cracked and put Adam in goal. We really didn't want to, but our desire to win toppled our sportsmanship a bit. Adam had grown up and played prominently in the city, so most people knew who he was and his goaltending history. It wasn't like Adam had full equipment on though. He had pads, a ball glove, a blocker and a back catcher's upper-body padding. It was the same stuff Noeller had used all day, but we hoped Adam's years of practice would be our, not-so-secret weapon.

This game was so different than the others. It was way more intense. There was more aggression going for the ball, fighting for space, and battling for loose balls. Although it never reached pugilistic behaviour, it certainly reached a level higher of aggression than we had experienced from any other team. MNP actually had the president of the local junior team playing. He was a big shot in the community because he was wealthy, active in the town, and he volunteered for the team. I knew him well. He was a good man. However, I found it a little intimidating facing off against him. Would this guy turn into a sore loser if we beat him? Would he stop running ads on the station? These were actual thoughts I had. Competition can change guys as I often saw with Noeller. He was a great guy 99% of the time, but if he was in a losing situation, he transformed into an incredible green rage monster.

This game against MNP had everything. Their goalie was quite good, the best we faced all day. They had good structure to their game, and they had guys who knew how to play. However, our new net-minder was doing his job. Adam was going save for save with their goalie, and when goals were scored, they were on scrambles in front. We were down 5-4 late in the game when I turned to "The Wand" for some magic. For years, I relied on my wrist-shot to get me goals in road hockey. Now I'm not going to compare my wrister to Joe Sakic's or anything pretentious like that. Burnaby Joe is a *Hockey Hall of Famer* and scored hundreds of goals with that patented wrist-shot. However, I'd like to think mine was one of the best among everyone I knew and played against over the years. It was pretty much how I scored most of my road hockey goals. I carried the ball over centre and began shifting to my left. I was a right-hand shot, and as I stepped further to the left wing, I skillfully lowered my right arm and flung the ball towards the net. The long move surprised the defence and the goalie as the ball zipped past everyone, far side into the net to tie the game up.

Once the game was equalized, neither team wanted to budge. The last couple of minutes were very conservative as we awaited overtime. I didn't know what would happen in a tie game, but soon found out - once time expired – that a shoot-out would be used to decide the winner. All three shooters on each team got one shot, and if things were still tied, then the team got to choose one person to shoot in a sudden death match. I went first. While running full speed, I saw the goalie come way out to challenge, so I faked a shot and sure enough, down he went. I then easily went around the fallen keeper and fired it into the empty net. MNP went next, and they scored. Noeller and Katherine both failed to score, but so did MNP's second and third shooters. It had come down to a sudden death shoot out.

My attitude had completely changed by this point. I felt intimidated before, but now I was full of confidence because I had scored our last two goals. For my second shot, I chose to do pretty much the same thing as the first. I ran in, but this time the goalie stayed deep in this net, not wanting to get deaked out like last time. I saw he wasn't coming out, and so I rifled a shot off the bar and in. Their goalie was caught totally off guard and was frozen when it went in. The only other time I had gotten really excited about a goal that day was after Katherine's game winner in our second game. I knew it wasn't polite to get too jacked after a goal, but I was pretty happy with this one. A few hard fist pumps escaped, but I stopped it before anything too greedy was released. After all, this was a charity event, and they still had their next shot coming up. I talked it over with Noeller and Katherine, and they decided, if MNP scored, I would shoot again for us. I wasn't looking forward to another shot because I was out of ideas. I probably would've just tried to snipe a corner, but I'm sure the goalie would be expecting that. I hoped Adam would save me from having to go out there again and try to pull off another goal. Their next shooter had scored earlier on Adam. He must have been watching me use speed to score because he also began to wind-up and get some momentum. However, Adam saw that the shooter was moving in fast. While the shooter kept his head down looking at the ball, Adam sprinted out of the net towards him and cut the angle down to almost nothing. When the shooter looked up, Adam was two feet in front of him and he had nowhere to go. His quick attempt was easily blocked and we won 6-5 in the shoot-out. We all jumped on top of Adam as waves of joy poured over us.

There was a little ceremony after the game where the other teams and those just watching the action helped us celebrate the win. Getting handed that big trophy was amazing! They had plates solidifying past winners, and now CKDM would be added to it. Sure enough, Noeller, Katherine and I took it back to the radio station and shared our victory with everyone in the office. Our afternoon jock first announced it, but when Noeller got the mic the next morning; he really pumped our tires. In between songs, Noeller told the story of our triumph and for the first time, I was being heralded as the clutch champion. I know it was only a small charity tournament, but it was great to win something. The fact that it was a title in road hockey made it feel like the greatest thing I'd ever done.

CHAPTER 13
Last Minute of Play

Years flew by. Jobs, families and this broad land has kept the guys and me from playing like we used to. Buff Dude, Coons and I were in the Prairies while Joel, Venkman, and Beezer still call southern Ontario home. I was in Ontario for a few months, in the fall of 2009, when a family member alerted me to a four on four road hockey tournament in Welland. It was an event to raise money for charity, so right away I knew it was not going to be a hardcore competitive tournament. Plus, there were no cash prizes; first place was a bunch of hockey sticks. Even though it had been years, I knew the guys would be right behind me. I eagerly contacted Joel, Venkman and Beezer, who willingly offered their support. Obviously, we needed more than four guys, so I called the few others I knew in the region.

My brother-in-law Bobby (I just call him Bobbo) used to play road hockey a lot, but like the rest of us, he hadn't played in some time, but he still joined in. One of

Bobbo's friends who I had gotten to know a little over the years was Glanfield. Glanfield was a tall dude with some power, and maybe the nicest guy ever. He was happy to play. Those two guys exhausted my resources. Neal was a definite no. Unfortunately, guys like Scott, Curly and The Doctor had faded from the picture long before, so I couldn't even call them. Luckily, Glanfield had a close friend who joined, as well as Joel's future brother-in-law. The eight of us entered the tournament as The Brantford Black Bears even though not a single one of us was currently living in Brantford. I couldn't resist!

Trips home to Ontario were always hectic. My wife's family is from Port Colborne, only about an hour away from Burlington, which was nice because we could easily visit both sides of our family when we do come. However, I have a big family, and there's always a parade of people to see which takes up most of my time. I did go home for Neal's wedding a few months before this, but I was only home for a couple days, so I couldn't see the guys. It had been over a year since I had seen Venkman, Joel and Beezer and wouldn't you know it, they were all at the rink, shooting around when I got there to see them again. What a fitting reunion... to play road hockey with the guys I had spent more time with than my family while in high school.

Joel had already suited up to play goal. For the first time ever, HE was ready before anyone else! Venkman had a sore back from his landscaping job, so he didn't think he should play goal. Besides, Joel had acquired much more goaltending experience over the years. After going to school in Toronto, Joel moved down to Louisiana and somehow found a men's rec league down there. Although I can't prove it, I imagine he was like Martin Brodeur down there to those guys. I can just picture him strolling into the rink, oozing with confidence. The hillbillies on skates probably leapt up and said, "I want him on my team, ya'll!" as they vied for his skills. Joel probably loved the attention and probably lived up the hype too. I'm sure he stole the show every game and solidified the reputation that Canadians are the best hockey players in the world.

I hadn't picked up a stick in years, and my shot had gone down the tubes. I used to be so proud of my wrist-shot. I could whip that thing with speed and precision, but now it was fluttering like an empty balloon. I had lost my best weapon and a good friend. Another knee injury – this time at work - earlier in the year had crippled the good wheels I developed in university so that part of my game was weak too. Street hockey was the only exercise I ever did. It helped me stay fit for years, but I hadn't played in so long that my cardio was garbage and I knew I'd be sucking wind soon. I laughed in my head at how out of shape my body had become, but I still had the drive! I knew I was going to have to use that will to get anywhere in this tournament. At least I wasn't alone. While Beezer, Glanfield, and Venkman were in good shape, the rest of us were below average. Based on our team's current state, I decided we needed a full-time defenceman, a couple rovers and a cherry picker.

The setup in Welland was really cool. They had outdoor rinks specifically created for road hockey. I had never seen anything like it. The rink was probably fifty feet long and thirty feet wide. It had four-foot high boards surrounding the facility with overhead lights, sheltered benches, and even a big score board. The surface was a kind of tile that helped the ball move quickly. We all liked the look of this place right away.

This tournament was different than the ones we used to play in. We automatically got another game because this was a three game elimination instead of two. Infractions would cost the guilty team two minutes of PK work instead of a penalty shot for the offended. There were a pair of ten-minute halves instead of one, continuous twenty-minute game. This allowed for a short intermission between periods, which was great for us because we really needed it!

With only eight players we couldn't have two full line changes, but we did our best. Bobbo and I played full-time D. Joel's, brother-in-law, Glanfield and Beezer roved while Glanfield's friend, and the ol' sniper (Venkman) cherry picked.

Our first test exposed our lack of cohesiveness. It took us some time to get used to playing together again. Meanwhile, it was clear that our opposition played together a lot. They exposed and countered our random running around with some solid passes and good scoring chances. We should have expected that none of us would play our best right off the get go. Thankfully, we got better which was encouraging. We lost 5-0, but all their scoring came in the first period. We knew we'd be better the next game, and we were.

By game two, we were very relaxed. We had improved by the second period of the opening game and were just getting better and better. Venkman was a superstar up front; Joel was really strong in goal, the rovers moved the ball well and I made some nice plays in my zone. Even after years of not playing, Venkman's shot hadn't suffered at all. He still had that fast, hard shot and a quick release. The other goalie had no answer for it. Venkman buried three of our eight goals. It was our second win as the Brantford Black Bears and easily our most productive game. I had one shot on goal in this game, and it wasn't much of one, but I wanted to contribute offensively. I always followed Don Cherry's advice and "put in on the net." However, my best biggest contribution to the team occurred on defence. I made a couple diving poke checks, broke up several passes and caught the attention of my teammates and the other team. My iron will was proving to be all I needed.

We were excited for game three because we had played so well in the previous game and won the match. The team we were about to play lost to the same team we did, but only on a late goal. It was a really entertaining game to watch! We stuck to our game plan but had to buckle down because this team had a lot of talented players. It was more intense than the previous games because we wanted to win so much more. Everyone was playing well as we exchanged goals. Joel was kickin' em out, but early in the second period, Glanfield went down with an ankle injury. Sadly, the shortest bench in the tournament got shorter. Glanfield had played well. He scored a goal and got some other opportunities, but he was hurt and could not return. I had my best scoring chance when I rushed (I'm using that term very liberally) down the right side and pulled it in for a shot, but got tripped up as I was shooting it. The play drew a penalty, but we didn't score.

With the game knotted at three in the second half; we started to get worn down. Venkman's back was acting up; Glanfield's friend took a shot off the toe that resulted in a limp, and the rest of us were just plain tired. I remember giving long looks to the bench for a change, but those who were already there were too tired to give up their spot. When the time to change did come, I was dogging it all the way off. Joel did a good job of watching out for those who needed to go off and for those who were most willing to sub on. Beezer had iron lungs. He played the most simply because he wasn't choking for air. He played the entire second half of that game without a break. I think that if we hadn't gotten so tired, we would've won. We played our best game of the tournament that contest. We fell one goal short in a 4-3 defeat. Again, we all felt good about our game. We played against a better team and we still kept them on their toes.

Our 1-2 record allowed us to play for the bronze which was very exciting because the Black Bears hadn't ever come close to winning a place on the podium before. To add to our good news, we were playing the team we had vanquished earlier in the day. Unfortunately, there was no time to rest for the game, so we knew we were in trouble. Bobbo was really hurting; he was just running on fumes by then. I think that if I hadn't wanted to play as much as I did, I would have been just as bad off as he was.

Things unravelled quickly in game four despite opening the scoring. Venkman was so sore, but still managed to let loose a "cannonading" shot that found the back of the net for his sixth of the day. He scored half our goals in the tournament. With the score 1-1, I went for another rush, but I stepped on a blade in traffic and dislocated my right knee again. Seeing my leg facing the wrong way was gross, and the pain was awful! My day was over. I pulled myself back to the bench, like a merman would on land. I felt bad, but there was nothing I could do. Our health problems cut our available roster down to five. Beezer and Joel's future brother-in-law were the only ones still in good shape. Venkman, Bobbo and Glanfield's friend were all suffering in some way, but they still played. These ailments meant we could barely put a team out there. Fatigue and injuries got the best of us, and we lost 6-1. The other team feasted on easy prey. They really let us have it after we had demolished them in our earlier contest. We took consolation in that fact that when we hit our stride and were healthy; we had a pretty good team.

The tournament turned out to be everything I expected. The other teams were really great; no one did, or said anything dirty or offensive. We talked to some of the guys after the games and found out that they played at this facility all the time in a league. Even though most of us were beaten up, we all agreed it was an enjoyable, fun day.

I saw Glanfield at a party a couple weeks after the tournament, and he was still on the mend. His ankle was still swollen, and he needed crutches. It turned out that he had torn a tendon in his ankle, but you wouldn't have known this at the time of the injury because he didn't even make a sound. I had my fourth knee surgery a couple months later back in Alberta.

That was the last time I played road hockey. It's been over five years, and there's no end to the drought in sight. Half of my years out west have been spent in Alberta. Alberta is one of Canada's lowest hockey-playing provinces. Most people I know in Alberta grew up playing football or basketball, and it shows. It was easy to find Tuesday night pick-up basketball. However, despite searching, I never found a place that plays floor hockey there (unless you're a student). Statistics show that 1.68%[1] of Albertans play organized ice hockey. That number lags behind seven other provinces! I'm not surprised by this. Ontario enjoys sheer bulk numbers that raise their grade. Ontario has the largest population in all of Canada. After living in both Manitoba and Saskatchewan for a combined seven years, I've seen how many people in small towns out here have the privilege of lots of ice time in their little rinks. Alberta does not have the giant population, nor the same proportion of small town rinks their Prairie brethren enjoy.

Next time we get together, hockey will be brought up for sure. Our wives know that for the rest of their lives, they're going to be hearing old road hockey stories as we relive them. It would be great to make some new stories, but they'll never replace the old ones. We played road hockey so much that we don't really have anything else to talk about from those days. Road hockey established our friendship and created our everlasting bond. No matter what happens, I know the boys will always be around to talk hockey with. We can go years without seeing each other and even months without talking, but somehow when we get together, it's like we can pick up right where we left off. We all have a truly remarkable relationship.

I always said that if I ever got rich I'd build a floor hockey rink and pay the guys to play all day. Not sure if our bodies would hold up like they used to though! Unfortunately, the chances of getting rich and doing that are slim to none, so we'll probably never find out. It's a sweet plan though.

CHAPTER 14
Setting Up My Soapbox

I never see kids or teenagers playing road hockey. Over the years and over the distances I've traveled across Canada, I've looked for people playing street hockey or at least evidence that games have been played. Maybe everyone plays floor hockey inside a gym, and no one plays street hockey anymore. Since leaving southern Ontario in 2000, I've lived all over the west, and it's the same story...no one outside playing road hockey. It could be a sunny, snow-packed November day, the kind of day you can toss your coat to one side and feel comfortable running around in just a sweatshirt, toque, and gloves. The kind of day that's cool enough to see steam leave your head when you take off your hat, but not so cold it hurts your face just to be outside. I look for kids out on days like those, and yet I still don't see anyone. I can remember looking out on a day like that and being so excited to play. I couldn't wait. I'd take my net out of the garage and escort it down the driveway to the road and just start shooting. Nobody else would be coming out for a while, but I just had to begin.

I used to feel this was an innate trait of all people born and raised in Canada, but I have to question that mentality now. Commercials selling hockey equipment and Canadian pride use clips of kids and adults playing road hockey in an effort to identify with the viewer. Perhaps it's used to evoke emotion for past generations, but I don't think it's accurate for the Z generation and up to today. I just don't see anyone playing anymore; therefore, making this marketing attempt quite invalid and inaccurate. Certainly, I understand that just because I don't see road hockey being played doesn't mean it's not happening. However, I've traveled a lot and lived in several different communities over the years, and haven't seen much evidence to counter the argument. Growing up, I remember seeing other kids out there, on different streets, in different parts of the city playing. If I could have, I would have jumped out of the car and started playing. That's not even possible now because there's nothing to jump out for. It really makes me sad to think my carefree road hockey days are dead, never to be resurrected. I wonder if I'll even be able to relive them with my kids.

As our road hockey days were wrapping up on Dante, at the end of high school in the summer of 1997, Venkman's neighbours had a kid who was probably ten and he and his friends would be outside playing road hockey. It made us feel happy thinking we inspired these kids to play. It was like we had passed the torch down to them. I'll always remember the day Pierre ran on the scene with Venkman and I. Since then, I've felt it would be great if I could do that. However, I just don't think I'll ever have the opportunity to. No one is out playing. Also, I'm afraid if I did join a game, parents these days would freak out and accuse me of pedophilia. This over protected society drives me nuts! We never saw Pierre as a potential creep or sex offender. He just wanted to play road hockey, and we loved it when he could. I can't grasp how some people believe those actions could be hazardous.

Thoughts of harm escaped us when we played street hockey. Aside from our goalies, we never even wore protection when we played. No helmets, gloves, shin pads or anything. If we got hit, slashed, tripped, cross-checked or hurt either by design or accident, we understood that, that was part of the game, and we soldiered on. We'd play all day on cold Saturdays throughout the winter and all night even with the threat of frostbite. We'd play with winter warnings in effect, during blizzards and deep freezes. Our goalies couldn't wear winter gloves when their hands were in the trapper, but they would happily exchange one frozen hand for a night of road hockey. We played during summer vacation when our goalies were sweating and battling heat exhaustion under layers of clothing. We never saw it as dangerous, our desire to play trumped everything else. I bet, now, parents would be wrapping their kids in foam rubber before they'd let them go outside to play road hockey.

I think playing street hockey developed a street sense in all of us. Watching out for cars, walking home in the dark every night after games and playing with guys we didn't really know (sometimes) somehow made us aware. In fact, I believe playing road hockey really rewarded my friends and I. No one ever did anything seriously criminal. None of us got mixed up with the wrong crowd, none of us got hooked on substances, none of us had to worry about depression, teen pregnancies, bullying, racism, suicidal thoughts or any of the plagues that lurked North American high schools. Road hockey helped us avoid these maladies. Our road hockey obsession protected us. It gave us purpose. It taught us goal-setting and organization. It fostered friendships, instilled happiness, and developed our mental and physical health. While reminiscing about these good times, I realized how much road hockey has shaped who I am today.

Epilogue
Stories too Good to Leave Out

In grade twelve, Ryan joined our group. Ryan was actually a guy I had grown up with. I remembered him from the many classes we had together since grade three. We were never close friends, but he and The Doctor had been friends for years. Once Ryan transferred high schools, he hung out with us all the time. Ryan was a good kid. He was super nice, but he was really needy. He clung to us like someone would clutch their last dollar.

Ryan had this old van that gave us a lot of freedom. After it got too dark to play road hockey, we'd still be up and want to do something. We'd all pile into Ryan's van and just drive. Sometimes that was all we would do. That van would magically whisk us away to places like Cambridge and Paris. Other times, we'd just do stupid stuff like driving fast through empty mall parking lots and ramming shopping carts to see how far they would fly off the bumper. We'd do drive-bys with water balloons, eggs and donuts. We would go to various fast food chains and collect condiments then use them as booby traps.

A single ketchup packet could do some decent damage when someone unknowingly stepped on it.

One of our favourite tricks was squeezing all of the filling out of jelly donuts onto an unsuspecting person's windshield wipers. During the summer evenings, we'd spread the filling on the wipers; then leave a few crumbs on the windshield. The driver would come back to his/her car, see the crumbs and use the wipers to clean them off. The jelly would then streak the windshield. It was awesome! I got Rit with that one once and he's still ticked off about it!

The best prank though was forking lawns. You need a few guys to pull it off, but it's a lot of fun when you do it. After acquiring a box of plastic forks, we'd go to someone's house at night. All of us would hop out of the van, and jam as many forks into the victim's lawn as we could in two minutes. The next morning, the owner would have to remove a hundred plastic forks from his/her lawn. Pulling all these pranks on people we knew was even more fun because we would hear them talking about it the next day. I was terrible at keeping these tricks a secret though. I'd start laughing my head off when I heard the story, and they'd immediately know it was me. We used the van for such stupid stuff, but we had a lot of fun doing it.

Ryan's van had a lot of memorable aspects to it. The gas tank was always on fumes, and when Ryan did put money into it, it was two dollars' worth. The rest of us would take the bus to school and a few times, we saw Ryan's van on the side of the road and knew it was there because it had run out of gas. Even though the fuel gauge was broken, you could hit a specific place on the dash to make the needle go up. We liked doing this because it gave us the illusion that there was more gas in the tank. In addition, there were egg stains on the ceiling for months. One time, I tried to chuck an egg out the door, but I accidentally hit the roof instead. Gooey egg landed all through the interior and all over us as well!

Perhaps we abused the van too much because it met its end on New Year's Eve in 1997. Everyone was meeting up for a party when Ryan was the last to arrive. I wasn't in the country, but the guys tell me Ryan simply opened the van's sliding door to grab some supplies, and the door fell right off! Beezer witnessed the whole thing and ran into the house where the guys were partying, yelling, "The door on Ryan's van just fell off!" Everyone came out to see it and died laughing. According to everyone there, Ryan sulked in a nearby field for the rest of the night.

The funniest story I've ever heard came from Coons and of course, it occurred in Ryan's van. One time, Coons and Ryan went to Buffalo for a Sabres game. Ryan didn't know squat about hockey, but he tried, just so he could fit in. They get to the rink and Coons had to pee badly. He couldn't hold it in, so he decided to take a leak into this empty, jumbo *Wendy's* cup that was in the van. Coons crawled into the back seat and began to fill 'er up. Before he knew it, a female parking lot attendant was at the window, asking them their business. As Coons tells it, "So, I've got this big cup of piss in one hand, and I'm trying to shove my schlong back into my pants with the other!" As his hands gesture his words, Coons had this big grin on his face that shared a look of both fright and excitement. Meanwhile, Ryan knew what was going on back there and was laughing so hard that the guard became curious and asked to look in the van. She did not see Mr. Winkie that night, nor did she force Coons to confess what was in the cup. I'm not sure how long this experience actually lasted, but I'm sure it felt like forever to Coons!

Endnotes

1   Hockey Canada's 2014 Annual Report. This document reports 9, 125 adults living in Alberta are registered in hockey. The author divided this number by the Statistics Canada 2014 population estimates (4.083 million) published following the 2011 Canadian Census.